KEEP OFF
MY TURF

KEEP OFF MY TURF

Mike Curtis with Bill Gilbert

WITH PHOTOGRAPHS

J. B. LIPPINCOTT COMPANY
Philadelphia and New York

U.S. Library of Congress Cataloging in Publication Data

Curtis, Mike, birth date
    Keep off my turf.

    1. Football.   I. Gilbert, Bill, birth date
II. Title.
GV954.C8   796.33'2   72–6128
ISBN–0–397–00895–3

*To the Millions of Americans
who enjoy Professional Football*

Foreword

Writing a book is not exactly my specialty. But under the circumstances I feel justified. The circumstances are these: There's too much anti-football sentiment in the air these days. A small handful of self-styled gridiron sociologists are trying to tell us how awful pro football is. Why, it's not only "degrading," they declare, it's downright "dehumanizing." I suppose next they'll be getting after me to change my nicknames. One of my nicknames is "Animal." The other is "Mad Dog." Somehow I don't feel dehumanized by either. What's more, I don't feel the least bit dehumanized when I take my place in the lineup against whatever team the Baltimore Colts happen to be playing on a particular Sunday afternoon. You see, I happen to be a professional football player who happens to *like* professional football.

Now in one respect I will have to agree with the critics of the game who after long and careful study have come up with the profound observation that, in the final analysis, football is a rough game. Of course it's a rough game. That's what makes football football and not backgammon. But it's also a great test of judgment, communicability and determination—in short, a microcosm of life itself. Dehumanizing? If it is anything, professional football is peculiarly human. If you don't think so, try to visualize eleven polar bears taking the field against eleven giraffes in a post-season game refereed by three kangaroos.

Anyway, I think it's time somebody stood up in defense of the sport and . . . well . . . as long as I'm standing . . . I just hope I don't have too much trouble switching, as a middle linebacker, from turf to paper. I also hope I don't come off sounding like some big-mouthed wise guy who thinks he knows it all simply because I'm angry enough to want to block all the inane kicking on the part of the critics. But that's the chance I'll have to take. It seems to me that the reason so many questions go unanswered—and so many problems remain unsolved—is that people too often hesitate to speak out because they are afraid of what others may think of them. So think what you will. I would be naïve if I did not expect to make some enemies. But if what I have to say helps to right some of the wrongs done professional football in recent years, maybe I'll also gain a few friends.

KEEP OFF
MY TURF

Chapter *1*

Dave Meggyesy isn't going to like this. That should make us even, because I don't like a lot of what he has to say. Johnny Sample is another who I'm sure won't go for what I have to say. Neither will Jim Bouton or Bernie Parrish. Because what I have to say is *pro* pro football, if you can imagine such a thing. For some reason—call it the tenor of the times if you want to—it has become fashionable for certain athletes to bite the hand that feeds them. And professional football seems to be the favorite chawstick. Yet tens of millions of Americans watch pro football every week during the season. There must be something good about a sport that brings so much excitement and pure fun to so many people.

But these days if an athlete has something good to say about his sport, it isn't considered news. Do you know why? Because it isn't controversial. That's the magic word. Publishers, for example, have found that they could sell more books by digging up some guy named Meggyesy or Bouton to rap football or baseball as hard as he could. The theory goes like this: the harder you rap, the more books you sell, the more money you make. It's curious how both Meggyesy and Bouton saw fit to raise holy objections to their professions after milking their respective sports for as much as possible in fat salaries for years. It's also strange that while these two men wrote the two books that made the most noise, neither of them was any great shucks in his sport. Bouton won eighteen or twenty-four games for the New York Yankees a couple of times, but that was back in the days when your grandmother could have done the same thing. Meggyesy never really made it big even with the St. Louis Cardinals, and, buddy, if you couldn't make it with the Cardinals in the years Meggyesy was with them. you had a problem.

So these two also-rans write books exposing their sports, after the money from the sports is safely tucked away in the bank or in their investment portfolios.

Pretty soon others are hopping on the same gravy train, and along comes Johnny Sample, washed up and released by the New York Jets and unwanted by any other football team, and he writes a book telling the youth of America to be dirty players. Then Bernie Parrish tells us that the whole business, which he engaged in for years, is either crooked or unethical or illegal or immoral, or all four.

And book firms publish this garbage and a lot of people

buy it and the money rolls in and that's supposed to make everything okay. Except that reality is distorted beyond recognition, and pro football comes out looking like the cause of everything from unemployment to cancer.

What if Meggyesy, for example, tried to take his case against pro football to court? Listen to the sort of pop he tries to peddle in his book *Out of My League:* that all you pro football fans follow the games on TV each week "in a sexual frenzy"; that the sport is responsible for our "militaristic" ways in the United States; that the President of the United States is a "football freak" whose fondness for the game is linked directly to "the most repressive political regime in the history of this country." What judge would allow such "evidence"? What jury would believe it? It's too bad Meggyesy can't take his case to court, because he wouldn't have a leg to stand on, and nothing would clear the good name of professional football quicker. Meggyesy is out of his league, all right.

As it is, professional football doesn't have to go to court to acquit itself. Millions of witnesses can testify to that—and have. All I want to do here and now, in my eighth year with the Baltimore Colts, is to add to that testimony . . . and let the game speak for itself.

The sweetest sound in the world is that of the gun that ends the game when your team is ahead in the Super Bowl. At first you can't believe your ears. Then a bullet of euphoria gets you right in the gut. Your legs become weak and you feel so giddy you want to roll in the turf from goalpost to goalpost. But you somehow manage to wade through the pandemonium on the playing field and into the mayhem of the locker room, where the bruises of the game are washed away in a flow of champagne, and you savor the taste of the ultimate victory. A beautiful way to end a season. . . .

And a far cry from the way the next one begins. Because on top of everything else, there is the burden of being the defending champions. After weeks of tortuous training plus six exhibition games and the College All-Star exercise, the championship mantle that felt so light in January seems to weigh a ton by July. And nobody has to remind you, as you get ready to plunge into the regular season slate of fourteen games, that it's one thing to win the title, but something else again to hold onto it.

Well, 1971 was not the best season the Baltimore Colts ever had. The fact that we didn't play better was especially frustrating to me, because in my opinion the 1971 team was superior to the 1970 team that won it all. For one thing, we had a more solid running game, especially with Norm Bulaich. It was only his second year, and he was already making a name for himself as a fast runner with incredible balance and drive. He's a real old-fashioned type of runner. He seems to take it as a personal offense when he's tackled. He won't miss a game unless you cut his legs off. That's a championship attitude.

We also had Don Nottingham, "the human bowling ball," the guy who runs so low to the ground they say the only way to bring him down is to hit him low—around the neck. And Don McCauley, a rookie from North Carolina who runs as well as a lot of veterans. And there was always Tom Matte, the ancient pride of Ohio State who came to the Colts so long ago he must be the only runner in the league eligible for Medicare. He's known as "the garbage runner." He does not have speed or do any

16

one thing in a great way, but he beats you anyway with "junk yardage," as Alex Karras once described it. Yet Matte gets his job done. He runs with his head and can make the big play like the old pro, which he is.

We had great receivers: John Mackey, just about the best tight end in football a couple of years ago, was still able to win for us, even though he was not a starter. And Tom Mitchell, young and good enough to replace Mackey as a starter, was a big plus factor. Eddie Hinton, with sticky fingers and great speed, was sure to be a key to our offense. I felt that he and Mitchell could make it or break it for our offense if our quarterbacks came through.

On defense we had more experience than we did in 1970. Ray May and Ted Hendricks had another year under their belts, and I had almost two seasons behind me as the middle linebacker after playing on the outside until mid-1969. People tell me that as a unit the Colts have the best set of linebackers in pro football today. I like to hear that, not out of vanity, but because if it's true, we're going to win some football games.

In playing between May and Hendricks I'm flanked by two of my favorite guys and two of our best players. May is coming fast after only a couple of years as a pro. He's a remarkable man, concerned enough to have adopted three kids who were in trouble. He spends nearly all his time—and damn near all his money—raising these kids by himself. Ray, you see, is a bachelor.

Ted Hendricks is "the Mad Stork." He's six feet, seven inches tall and weighs only 218 pounds. When he intercepts a pass or runs from his position to close in on the play, those long, skinny legs are flapping every which way and he really does look like a mad stork.

Jerry Logan, Rick Volk, Jim Duncan and Charley Stukes gave us a solid defensive backfield. I was confident that both our offensive and defensive lines could do the job.

And yet we didn't do well at all in the exhibitions. It was win one, lose one, win one, lose one—world champions just hobbling along. We didn't seem to be pushing ourselves. It all seemed to boil down to the quarterback position. Earl Morrall, at age thirty-seven, just couldn't seem to get going, and John Unitas was still recovering from an off-season heel injury. Either would have to start performing—and soon. During the exhibition season the tendency is to say there's still time to straighten things out. But I think that's the wrong attitude. Exhibitions help set a frame of mind that brings about a team's cohesion. Besides, I never accept defeat, even when it doesn't count. That way I won't accept it when it does count. I kept hoping the guys would shape up.

One of the "fringe" benefits that goes to the team that wins in the Super Bowl is that they get to play the College All-Stars in the preseasonal rites. Our game against the All-Stars was something of a joke. The game usually is. There's only one reason why the annual event shouldn't be discontinued: In thirty-seven years this game has raised over $9 million for more than 100 charity organizations. If it weren't for that, I'd vote to discontinue it. Most pro players consider it a waste of time. What with their tight training schedule, it's tough for the pro players to get up for this game. But they manage anyway, more out of pride than eagerness. And it's no easier on the college players. They have three weeks to get ready, and that's just not enough for a team of all-strangers to become cohesive. They are too disorganized. All they can do is pass, unless it's a year when they have a great runner like Gale Sayres or O. J. Simpson. Those years don't come often. They're not the best players in the country anyhow. They may have been the best last year—in college—but they don't even belong on the same field with the pro champions, regardless of who the champs are.

Anyway, the game doesn't thrill me as much as it used to, and I don't think it's because I've been playing pro ball for eight years. And I have a feeling the fans aren't as excited about this "classic" as they used to be, either. It's just not the attraction it once was. It's a risky game, too. The college players might get hurt and ruin their chances of making the grade in the pros. And the pro players might get hurt and put themselves out of action.

In one respect the 1971 Colt team was different from previous Colt teams: we didn't have as many clowns as we did a few years back. Guys like Alex Hawkins, Billy Ray Smith, Jim Parker, Dick Szymanski, Ordell Braase and Jimmy Orr were all cutups.

When I was a rookie third-string fullback in 1965, I always wore the same old clothes. I still do. That's my way. I'm not a fancy guy, and I'll wear khakis or dungarees and a tee shirt and white socks and boots whenever I can. Alex Hawkins got so tired of seeing me in the same getup every day he once staged a solemn ritual and burned my socks. Right there in the middle of the dressing room. And they call *me* The Animal and Mad Dog?

We used to have rookie shows in training camp and all the rookies were made to do stupid, silly things, usually in the nude. I refused. The shows were absolutely gross, so I just said I wasn't going to participate. The day I was supposed to appear I went home instead. The veteran players told me they would get me, but I said I didn't care, I wasn't going to put up with that crap, and I didn't. I dared anybody to do something about it. Nobody did.

This year's Colts are a happy club with no troublesome guys, no tough white rednecks or tough strident blacks. We don't have any clubhouse lawyers. We had some in the past, but they're gone now, and in each case it was no accident. We visit in each other's homes, we go out together, we go to church together. All in all, we live a pretty close life, content in each other's company, from July until December or January—January if we're lucky.

But to me the thing that really counts is winning. I think we're one of the best teams in pro football, if not *the* best. We've been winners for years, and that is now a tradition with the Baltimore Colts. We've built it up into Yankee-like proportions. But we can't expect it to continue automatically. We have to play hard as hell and hit hard as hell for that winning tradition to continue, and for the money that comes with it.

And we still have one or two scores to settle. There was that defeat by the Jets in the 1969 Super Bowl. We had hoped to avenge that in 1971. Instead we came up against the Dallas Cowboys. And then when we won it, the armchair analysts shrugged and said we hadn't beaten a very good team. So we have to prove ourselves all over again.

We opened the 1971 season on a high note, creaming the New York Jets, 22–0, in a downpour. It's always a pleasure to down the Jets after that awful, awful loss to them in the Super Bowl following the 1968 season. We haven't lost to them since, and it figures. But nobody seems to take stock in such facts. All they know is that the Jets whipped us in one of the most stunning football upsets of all time. But that was a hundred years ago.

We wanted this one in the worst way, and we played better than we had all through the exhibition season. The guys were tensed up something fierce. I noticed at the pre-game meal that many looked nervous and pensive. And this was four hours before the game.

You never know how to interpret that. I've seen players look that way before a game and then go out and lose it through sloppy play. And I've seen them laughing and clowning around before a game in which they wiped up the field with the other team. You never know. But even the coaches were uptight before the Jet game, and the head man himself, Don McCafferty, gave us a talk, which he doesn't usually do. It was all blood-and-guts stuff that you've seen in movies—you know, get out there and whip their butts off . . . this isn't any of that preseason crap . . . go out there to win . . . they're trying to take the bread off our table. I guess some guys respond to that sort of thing. I don't need it. I'm always ready to play.

Norman Bulaich was as tense as anyone. I drove to the game with him and right after we got to Memorial Stadium he threw up his guts. Then, after hurting his ankle in the first quarter, he went out and gained 198 yards. The Associated Press named him Offensive Player of the Week. Lucky for the Jets he had an upset stomach and a bad ankle. Too bad he couldn't have gained two more yards. Two hundred yards sounds better.

I was satisfied with my own performance in helping to get the shutout. I felt I made my share of tackles and busted up enough plays to help stop them. The main thing was I'd gotten enough sleep, which is extremely important to me. I can't perform without it. A good night's sleep acts like a Dexedrine pill and picks me up and I feel great, as if I can do everything I want.

All in all, I was encouraged by our showing against the Jets. I had been very upset after our exhibition season, in which we won three and lost four and looked lousy. The guys were too casual, and the coaches didn't jump on us enough for our mistakes, including me. But that's not McCafferty's style. He's soft-spoken and easygoing, and maybe that way works best for him.

My own preference is for the tough disciplinarian, the Vince Lombardi or Don Shula type. Professional athletes need to be handled in a tough way. They're not getting those high salaries for being thin-skinned, especially when the criticism is intended to make them better at their profession and thus able to earn more money. I never enjoyed having Shula scream at me, but I knew he was making me a better football player. The other way doesn't work, and you don't win. That's the Dr. Spock school of coaching.

When Otto Graham was coaching the Redskins, I once saw him walk over to a player who had just missed a punt and put his arm around him. Man, you don't get anywhere that way. If I were a coach and one of my players missed a play, I'd walk over and shake his damn shoulders and force him to make the play right the next time. Both the player and the team would be better off for it.

So we beat the Jets and we had a day off to lick our

wounds and on Tuesday we started getting ready for our upcoming game against the Cleveland Browns. This game had more than passing significance for us, because Cleveland figured to be one of the teams we'd have to beat out for the American Conference title. And we knew they'd be plenty high for us because we clobbered them in 1968, 34–0, on our way to the Super Bowl.

Leroy Kelly was running well and that was bad news. Kelly has never been one of my favorites—not since the 1968 season. That year he was voted one of the all-pro running backs by NEA news service. I was in the audience when he received his award at a dinner preceding the Pro Bowl. He hardly thanked the people at all. Instead, he said, "I'll see you next year to pick up my award again." That was bush. You don't say things like that if you're a champion.

Another criticism I have of Leroy Kelly is that he doesn't block, and I'm not the only player who feels that way about him. He's like one of his Cleveland predecessors, Bobby Mitchell. Mitchell didn't block much either when he was a running back with the Browns or when he was a receiver with the Redskins. The consensus in the league was that he did not help his team that much overall. He was a great runner and he moved well, but he seldom blocked and quite often he did not run out his patterns on a pass play if the pass was to another receiver.

I once saw Mitchell catch a pass and break into the clear and head for the goal line. Just then an opponent came toward him on an angle to knock him out of bounds. He was about ten yards away from Mitchell. Mitchell could have had a touchdown. Instead, he stepped out of bounds to avoid getting hit, and the play was over. Leroy Kelly seemed to suffer from a similar syndrome when it came to blocking.

But like him or not, we gave Mr. Kelly and company our fullest attention that week. Our preparation, similar to the routine we were to follow each week throughout the season went like this:

Tuesday: Viewed films of the previous Sunday's game with the Jets and evaluated our performances. Nobody felt bad about that one. Still, there were lessons to be learned. After that we loosened up and ran "gassers." Four sets of four players sprint the width of the field and back. We call them gassers because they make you run out of gas. Following that, the quarterbacks left for the club's offices in Baltimore to study for the next game.

We also learned that Bulaich had been named Offensive Player of the Week by the Associated Press. No one made much of a fuss about it, but you could bet he'd remember it at contract time. Players have long memories on things like that. Raymond Berry was one who really played it to the hilt. He'd come into the Colts' front office at contract time armed with more information about his performance the preceding season than the Colts knew themselves. He kept it all in a notebook—how many catches, yardage gained, touchdowns scored, third-down plays made, everything. (But then, anyone who put flowers in his room and curtains on his window in training camp could be expected to be that thorough.) He had it worked out just how much each catch the previous year was worth, a dollar value for every one. It would be hours before he would come out of the office during his contract talks. If you were visiting the front office for the same reason, you could just plan on coming back the next day.

Wednesday: Offensive day. We reported at 10 A.M. and got a rundown on each opposing player—his height and weight, what he did and didn't do well and ways to take advantage of the other team's weaknesses under given conditions. We then got our plans for the week—what defenses we'd run, what coverages we'd use. We studied the other team's pass patterns as well as their running plays, noting which side they like to run on. The skull sessions usually last for two hours. We got taped, had lunch and saw a film of our opponents' latest game. After that we practiced for an hour and a half, staging the opposition's defenses for our offense to run against.

Thursday: Defensive day. On the practice field at 12:30. After a team meeting, we broke up into offensive and defensive teams. Another look at game films, before returning to the field for our workout.

About those practice facilities at the McDonough Boys' School in suburban Baltimore. It's a beautiful setting, but lousy for a football team. The facilities are 300 yards from the playing field. The training room is about twenty by fifteen feet, with two tables and equipment and medicine for forty-five guys. There is one commode and one urinal and no partitions. It isn't exactly the major leagues, and not what you might expect of practice facilities for world champions. It's a steel stadium and the windows have been welded shut because of break-ins (even in suburbia). The whole place was built in the 1930s and it's hotter in our dressing room than it is out on the field. As a result, we get a steam bath before we begin our workout.

We finished at around 3:30, after a mock game in which we tested our defenses against what we expected from our opponents.

Friday: Weigh-in at 12:30. You get an assigned weight when you join the Colts and they expect you to maintain that weight throughout the years unless otherwise notified. Mine is 235 pounds, which is reasonable for my height of six feet, three inches. For every pound you're overweight, you're fined ten dollars for each day you stay overweight. The money goes to Kernan's Children's Hospital in Baltimore. They get a couple of thousand bucks a year from us in player fines, not only from overweight players, but also from those who break curfew, come late to meetings, or behave in a manner unbecoming the Baltimore Colts. We could take the dough and use it for a blast of a party, but we give it to help the kids in the hospital instead. (Dave Meggyesy, please note.)

Saturday: We came in at 10:30, went over our kicking game and were through by noon. So much for Saturday. Pro football is deceiving, though. You may not spend too much time in actual practice or in meetings, but you spend many hours thinking about it at home and preparing yourself and shutting yourself off from your wife while you go over your book for the next game.

Against us Sunday, from all indications, Cleveland would try to give the ball to Leroy Kelly a lot. If we could stop him, we would stop Cleveland. I noticed again in the Cleveland films that Kelly still wasn't blocking. He must have picked that up from Jim Brown as well as from Bobby Mitchell. Meggyesy says all the criticism against Brown for his blocking was racism. The hell it was. It was simple fact. And the criticism was never that Brown *couldn't* block. It was that he *wouldn't* block.

Cleveland likes to run a lot of sweeps with Kelly and a lot of quick openers up the middle. I had to be aware of that. If I could stop the middle, we'd be all right. Curtis was ready for Kelly.

Chapter 2

I ended that Kelly-Curtis duel in a hurry—by breaking my thumb. I got hurt in the first quarter, and so did Norm Bulaich, who reinjured his ankle, and neither one of us came back in the game. To make matters worse, we lost to Cleveland, 14–13. But the real reason we lost was that we gave the Browns the ball eight times on fumbles and interceptions. And still they beat us by only one point.

I broke the thumb on a play in which Bill Nelsen threw a flare pass to Leroy Kelly coming out of the backfield. I ran over to hit him, but I didn't knock him down completely. He stumbled for a few more yards. I ran into his hip with my head and it made me dizzy. But when I swung my right arm around to hook him, his left leg came up and jammed into my right thumb. I had never noticed before that he hits hard when he's running, and that he doesn't usually run with his knees high. Just my luck he was running both hard and high on that play.

The thumb turned blue, but I thought it was a broken blood vessel or a bruise. On the next play I found I couldn't use that hand, and I had to make a one-handed tackle. So I took myself out of the game. Despite my animal and mad dog image, I don't believe in playing when you're hurt if it doesn't help the team.

They took me to the hospital and operated that evening. In addition to resetting the thumb, they had to put two steel pins in it, because it was bent back when it broke and kept popping out of place. Eventually, the pins gave me an advantage, though. They helped the broken bone to mend faster and stronger.

I left the hospital Monday. Would you believe it, I had a contractual commitment for four hundred dollars to appear at an autograph session that day? Despite the pain shots I was taking, that thumb just about killed me. But I felt I had to go through with it. You do what you have to do.

And so, what had looked like a promising season was now bent into the shape of a question mark. I would have plenty to think about as I sat on the bench for who knew how many games.

After two games it was rapidly becoming apparent that the Colts were a team in transition. We had been riding to championships for years on the arm and the brain of John Unitas, supplemented by a good running game. But the passing of Unitas had been the key. Now John was thirty-eight and still recovering from that heel injury. Morrall, at 37, was slow getting started and just wasn't hitting his receivers. At the same time, our running game was dominating our offense, and not just because of Earl's slump. I think Norm Bulaich very soon will be the best runner the Colts have ever had—if he isn't already—and that includes Alan Ameche and Lenny Moore. He's got the good moves and the ballet dancer's balance of a great runner. And Matte, Nottingham and McCauley are all good enough to play regularly on any other team. It might have happened that the running game would take over as the primary part of our offense even without the troubles of Unitas and Morrall, but whatever the immediate cause, the Colts were now primarily a running team supplemented by its passers.

That's like the Yankees becoming a singles team like the White Sox after all those years as a home run team. But I think the switch will work better for us than it did for the Yankees. Our runners are good enough to be our main offensive weapon and win for us.

Part of the quarterback problem is loyalty. The Colts are a loyal organization. They'll stay with you if you've delivered for them over the years. Many guys have played ten or twelve years with the Colts, and the Colts have stuck with them rather than get rid of them the minute they start to age.

Unitas is the current example. He won the first championship for us in 1958. He's won a flock of everything for us ever since, so we'll still go with him. Earl has been with us only since 1968, but the same thing applies to him.

He stepped in for Unitas that year, got us the NFL championship and won himself the NFL Player of the Year Award. Then in January, 1971, he stepped in again in the Super Bowl after John got hurt and helped us win the world title. So the Colts won't cut Earl loose either—not yet anyway.

As if my enforced idleness weren't depressing enough—they said I'd be out for three or four games—I found myself thinking more and more of all the lies and distortions that were being pushed by the many critics of professional football today, and of the many people who would be reading, believing and unwittingly spreading such untruths. If, as they say, the truth never catches up with the lie, then pro football is in real trouble. But someone has to try to pull the truth up out of the quicksand.

Sample's book could have been amusing if not for the serious goof he makes in bragging about being a dirty player and encouraging today's kids to do the same. I can give kids some advice on that: Don't. Look at Sample's own career. He wasn't all that great, but maybe he could have been if he had concentrated on playing the right way.

Boastful as he is about foul play—and that's supposed to make you think he was tough—the case he tries to make for himself is a joke to anyone who played when he did. In his book he tells how he dared our receivers to tangle with him in our Super Bowl game against the Jets. He says they didn't, and that meant they didn't have the guts to take him on. That's ridiculous. They just didn't have the stomach to play as dirty as Johnny Sample. That's all there was to it. Who the hell wants to stoop as low as Sample does?

When Sample came into the league, he was a better than average player, but after a while all he wanted to do was mouth off. He never seemed to care about executing his defenses the way he was supposed to. He was a football player, not a professional.

When Sample was with the Redskins, it was no secret that he would get beaten like a drum on pass plays all day, then come up with an interception once in a while. At best, his interceptions merely neutralized his mistakes. He was always getting beaten for touchdowns. We used to run all over him.

Sample spends his whole damn book telling how he was always getting a bum rap. I'd be interested in knowing what it would have taken for Sample to be happy during his pro career. Maybe he thought he was worth $100,000 a year. He played with four teams and he wasn't happy with any of them. And they all got rid of him.

He reminds me of the baseball story my Washington friends tell about a guy named Mickey McDermott who used to pitch for the Red Sox, Senators, Yankees and a few other teams and who never really made it. When the Yankees unloaded him, he complained he never got the chance to pitch much. It was Casey Stengel who said, "All I know, son, is that four other managers gave you a chance to pitch, and they all got fired."

Sample says that he played dirty because he was aggressive, and that he always played that way. Baloney. The fact is that Sample played dirty because he was *not* aggressive. He couldn't compete with the rest of the players

32

on their level, so he had to do it by hitting them in the neck or punching them in the back.

I have a reputation for being an aggressive player, too, and a rough one, and so do Dick Butkus and Willie Lanier, but I don't think we have a reputation for being dirty players. Sample did. He always did. He must have been proud of it if he used it for the title of his life's story: *Confessions of a Dirty Ballplayer*. Isn't that something to be proud of?

I'm sure some kids will try to pattern themselves after Sample, because that's what kids do. They model themselves after their heroes, and ballplayers are their heroes. But those kids will find out they're just going to get hurt if they play Sample's way.

Fortunately, the ones kids imitate most are the stars. It's interesting that very few stars write books attacking their sport. The players who do are the malcontents on the fringe of fame. And they're usually better known for their books than for anything they ever did on the field.

I wonder what some of the veteran Redskins are going to say when they read what he said about Sonny Jurgensen. He says Jurgy isn't an intelligent quarterback. I don't know how he came to that conclusion. Whenever we play the Redskins, our coaches tell us to disguise our defenses, because Sonny can read defenses better than any other quarterback in football. Sample questions Sonny's ability to call a good game. But if coaches on other teams also think he's the best there is at reading defenses, then he must be able to call a good game as well. Once again, Sample doesn't know what the hell he's talking about.

He goes on at great length about how sure the Jets were they would beat us in the Super Bowl following the

1968 season. But the Jets players themselves tell me they were hoping to get off the field without getting embarrassed against us.

Sample says Weeb Ewbank didn't have control of the club, because Joe Namath, Emerson Boozer and Matt Snell didn't show up one day for publicity pictures. What kind of flimsy evidence is that? They got into the Super Bowl and they won, so somebody must have been in control.

During that game Sample intercepted a pass against us and then shoved the ball into Willie Richardson's face coming off the field. No reason. He just shoved it into Willie's face. Another time Willie ran out of bounds and Sample came up and clubbed him. But Sample fails to mention these things in his book. All he says is that Tom Mitchell came up swinging at him with his helmet from the Colts' bench, which was true, but he doesn't bother to mention the other things that prompted it.

The Samples and the Meggyesys of pro football are proving a point without knowing it. They are a mirror of malcontents, and this seems to be the age of the malcontents. Sure there are conditions in pro football that could stand changing. There are conditions in every segment of American society that could stand changing. But if it is to be changed for the better, it had best come through the sound and reasonable efforts of sound and reasonable men.

Pro football is, after all, a microcosm of America in the 1970s. It's a fast sport, and Americans travel at a fast pace. There is violence, and Americans, admit it or not, like violence—at least in their sports. There is great affluence and maybe there are certain injustices. Maybe that's why pro football is so popular—because it's so much like the rest of American society.

Two days after the Cleveland game I was at odds with myself, wanting to play in the worst way, but at the same time realizing that if I came back too soon, I'd be risking even more serious injury that could put me out for the whole year.

It's always that way when I get hurt. In my junior year at Duke I hurt my knee, which kept me from playing in our big rivalry against North Carolina in the final game of the season. All the coaches, except the head coach, Bill Murray, were down on me because I kept insisting my knee just wasn't ready. They wanted me to play because it was Carolina. But if I had played and made the injury worse, I might have missed my last year of college football. I might also have missed out on my pro career and maybe left myself with a bum knee and a limp the rest of my life. Because I was unwilling to take such a gamble, some people I believed to be my friends suddenly turned out not to be.

Dave Meggyesy and I find ourselves at opposite ends on the subject of injuries. He says that during his playing days at Syracuse it would have required courage to tell the coach you were hurt and wouldn't play until your injury healed. I don't think it takes any more courage than it did at Duke. It just takes common sense. That doesn't mean I'm the kind of player who goes around worrying about getting hurt. You can't play full tilt that way. No, I don't worry *about* getting hurt. I worry *after* I get hurt—about how soon I'll be back.

Anyway, the thumb continued to prey on my mind, and I knew how frustrated I would be for the next week or two. At first it was something of a relief to know I wouldn't have to cope with the tension or disappointment over our inconsistent performances. But the anxiety soon got to me, and I began asking people how I could get the swelling down and the pain reduced faster so I could come back sooner. I even found myself thinking I must get ready for the upcoming game with the Patriots.

Chapter *3*

In our third game of the season we beat the New England Patriots, 23–3, at their new stadium in Foxboro, Massachusetts. It wasn't much fun for me, though. All I could do was pace up and down the sidelines in street clothes, with that stupid cast on my thumb. It was the first game I'd missed since my knee operation in 1967.

The trip to Foxboro was more eventful than the win. On the flight up from Baltimore to Boston we hit an air pocket and plunged a hundred feet in a split second. Then it seemed as if the engines cut out. We made a dead stick landing, and by that time a lot of us were willing to take the train to our next game in Buffalo.

When we hit that air pocket, the stewardess was serving milk and soft drinks. Her tray hit the ceiling and she hit the deck. Bob Vogel was sitting in front of me drinking milk. All of a sudden the carton was in the air and he was trying to catch it like a receiver trying to gain possession of a juggled pass. I grabbed my seat belt with my good hand and hooked it together—fast. The disturbance was part of a storm associated with Hurricane Ginger. The incident never hit the papers, but we were all scared, especially after the engines cut out.

When I get hurt and knocked out of action, I have to fight hard to ward off depression. So I keep reminding myself how lucky I am. Doing what I want to, making good money, enjoying a certain degree of success and recognition. You've got to be pretty selfish to ask for any more than that, or half as much. It's a satisfying feeling to look back on it all and think about all those "insurmountable" obstacles you somehow managed to hurdle. . . .

I remember the first time I got my name in the paper. That was back in Richard Montgomery High School in Rockville, Maryland, thirty minutes out of Washington, D.C., in suburban Montgomery County, where things got started for me in the late 1950s. We beat Suitland High School, a school over in the next county, and for some reason my name was in the story about the game in the *Washington Star*. I can't even remember what it said about me. I just know that seeing my name in print in a Washington paper was about the most exciting thing that could ever happen to a sixteen-year-old kid. I grabbed it and hurried to my Dad, who was hanging around the house with me that Saturday afternoon and said, "Look at this,

Dad! I got my name in the paper! Durn, Dad, that's pretty neat!"

But just to show you that publicity is not everything, we wound up the year with two wins and eight losses. Adversity is a great leveler. The publicity continued, and it produced at least one change in our family. My sister Karen came to be known by the initials MCS—Mike Curtis' Sister.

In my junior year we got a new football coach, Roy Lester, who later became head coach at the University of Maryland. The first time I talked to him he was issuing uniform numbers and he said, "What number do you want, Curtis?"

I said, "I don't know. Just give me any number."

Lester said, "How would you like to have the number of a great fullback at Maryland?"

I told him I guessed that was okay, so I got number forty-one. I still don't know who number forty-one was that year at Maryland. Hell, I didn't even know where the University of Maryland was, even though it was only a half-hour from my home. That's how small an orbit I traveled in. But Lester must have known what he was doing. We went undefeated that year.

I was named the high school player of the week by the *Washington Post* that year, but I was even prouder when I made the honor roll for my school work. I had to work harder for that. It was the same kind of greater pride in scholastic work than in football accomplishments that carried over to my college days at Duke.

It was in high school that I first felt frustration and extreme anger if I wasn't playing the way I should and helping the team, or if the team itself wasn't playing well.

We were playing Northwestern High School, and on one of our running plays the lineman running interference for me wasn't getting out in front fast enough to suit me, so I screamed at him as we started to sweep the end, "Come on, dammit! Move! Go!" I had never talked to a teammate like that before, certainly not while a play was going on. I always ran and blocked aggressively, but I never thought of myself as particularly aggressive until that one play. Then I sensed that I was changing into a fierce ballplayer. I don't know what that said for my ability, but I know what it said for my attitude. I was ready to take on the world if it meant winning a ball game. That's been my attitude ever since.

As a senior, I was lucky enough to be voted to the All-Metropolitan team of high school players in the Washington area, and then came the icing on the cake. I was named the area's outstanding football player of the year. I even got to wear a tux when I received my award at the Washington Touchdown Club banquet in January, 1961. Like most winter sports affairs, this is always a big bash, and I found myself at the head table—at the head table!—with Whitey Ford and Mickey Mantle and a lot of other stars. I remember thinking: "What the hell am I doing here? Where's the door?"

I was too embarrassed to ask anyone for an autograph. I just stood back behind the curtain somewhere most of the time, sort of hiding and gawking at all those famous faces. It was a dream, I was sure of that. When I got my award, I thanked them with the worst speech anyone ever had to listen to and left as soon as possible. Dad went with me, and I remember hugging that trophy all the way home while he drove. I didn't want anything to happen to it.

In my senior year a lot of guys began coming around to recruit me for college. I still had only a hazy idea of where the University of Maryland was located, and I hadn't really given the subject of college much thought. But others had. Dad wanted me to go to the University of Virginia. He once had a chance to go there on a baseball scholarship and didn't take it. But I was partial to Navy. I was quite taken with all that military stuff. I never even thought about scholastic requirements. But I always wanted to be an engineer, because I thought that would make Dad happy and maybe the Naval Academy would give me that opportunity.

The people at Navy took me to the Army-Navy game, drove me up there and back. Meanwhile, I had been getting a lot of letters, and I wanted to check out every possibility. Dad and I went to the University of Tennessee and they showed us the engineering department, and I wasn't impressed at all, especially by its location in the basement of a building. The players seemed like a bunch of animals at dinner at the training table. I just wasn't impressed.

Then Syracuse University, the school that gave the world Dave Meggyesy, entered the picture. One of their representatives contacted Dad, who was handling everything for me, and he offered Dad a car for me but Dad turned him down. He didn't tell me about the car until later, because he didn't want me to be influenced by that. He knew what he was doing. If I had known it at the time, I would have gone to Syracuse in a minute.

That was the second time my parents had intervened in my behalf without my knowledge. The first had been while I was still playing football for Montgomery High and I came home from practice one day and said, "Boy, Mom, that Coach Lester sure hollers at me a lot."

He never did after that, and the reason didn't occur to me. Nine years later I found out she had called Lester up and told him to quit picking on her little boy.

All I knew about the Syracuse offer was my impression of their representative. He wore a mustache that was uneven and he had a grease spot on his tie. I never considered Syracuse after seeing that guy.

Duke invited me to visit its campus. The first time I saw it I thought it was beautiful. The assistant athletic director, Carl James, escorted me around and made me feel right at home, a feeling I had not experienced on my visits to other campuses. He was smart enough to include his wife and their two little girls in our group, and everyone was friendly to me and I felt comfortable in their midst. While they were showing me around I decided to enroll there. Then I found out it was a damn good school, too.

I might have visited the University of California to look the school over, but they told me I had to sign a letter of intent. To me that meant a commitment to go there, and I wasn't about to do that before seeing the place, so I didn't do it. I also heard from Alabama and Texas and what seemed like a million other colleges, but it was Duke for me.

My freshman year in college was sheer tragedy. I was so lonesome that the world came crashing in on me every day that year. I'm not the letter-writing type, but I turned out seven letters a day for the first three weeks I was away from home. I had never been separated for so long a time or distance from my family, and I was as homesick as the rawest Army recruit. I wouldn't have wished that year on my worst enemy, and not just because I was homesick. That turned out to be only the tip of the iceberg.

I had no friends, knew no one and I even went to church every Sunday—something I never did back home. On Saturdays everyone would go down to watch the varsity team play, but I would just stay in my room. I was afraid to go out, but I didn't want to stay in, so there I was. Sometimes I would go to a movie—if I had enough money. But mostly I just listened to the radio and stared at the walls.

I played on the freshman team and hurt my knee and broke a bone in my hand. It was that kind of a year on the field, and later I discovered it had been that kind of a year in the classroom as well.

Christmas came around and I knew I had a lot of studying to make up for all the time I spent playing football that first semester. So I went home with high resolve to hit the books and then said the hell with it. I just ran around with my old high school buddies and my girl friend and enjoyed being alive again after three months of pure hell in my self-imposed isolation at Duke. I spent a lot of time with my best friend, Kenny Tuchtan, whose father was later mayor of Rockville. His name is Achilles Tuchtan (pronounced tuck-ten, with the accent on the first syllable). He's the only mayor ever to be introduced at a sports banquet as "the Honorable Achilles Tendon."

When final exams rolled around, the world caved in on me all over again. I knew I was in trouble, but I never dreamed how much. I didn't know my calculus from my humerus, my French was a foreign language—especially to a Frenchman—and the inside of my zoology lab was a strange jungle to me. I had never done any homework, because I never had the time or the strength after football practice. And I had never taken notes in class, because I figured all that stuff was in the textbook.

We had a week and a half just to take final exams. I thought, "What the hell, I'll do what I did at Richard Montgomery. I'll just put in a couple of hours the night before and I'll be ready." So I started studying. . . .

The first exam was in calculus. They handed out the final and I opened it up and thought, "Oh my God!" I must have been reading the wrong book the night before, because I sure as hell didn't see anything in that exam that looked familiar to me. The guy in front of me is writing like mad and all of a sudden he's finished and gone. Then others started to get up and leave and nobody seemed to be having the cold sweat that I was.

I got an F in that course.

The next exam was zoology. I started to prep for it the night before, looked at the book and said, "Hell, I'll never learn all this in one night." So I closed the book and turned on the radio. I was so far out of it I didn't have the vaguest idea of what was going on in that course, either.

I got another F.

Then came French. I whipped open the book the night before in hopes of absorbing something. When I entered the classroom the following morning ready to conjugate the verbs I knew, the professor was talking in French, and I didn't understand one damn word. Then he saw the blank expression on my face and addressed me in English: "Mr. Curtis, I've been telling you to put your name on the paper."

I got my third F.

Well, English always responded to my efforts, and history always came easy, so I knew I could make a comeback of sorts with those subjects. My English prof asked me if I had my poem ready and I said "Yessir" and he said, "That's wrong. That's not the correct work." So I got a D in English.

Now I was sure I knew my history because I had studied. But I got a D anyway because by this time I was so rattled I had no idea of what the hell I was doing in anything. I bailed myself out with an A in Physical Education. I knew I had flunked out. Then I got the word—I was on probation. I had to make a 1.5 average in my second semester. And my report card was sent home, showing that the pride of the Curtis household had knocked 'em dead at Duke with F, F, F, D, D—and one A.

It was one of the best things that ever happened to me. I realized then that the most important thing in my life was to graduate from college. Nothing else, including football, was important. Even my girl friend had to shape up or ship out in my new scale of priorities. I told her either we do things this way and I'm free to concentrate on my studies, or we split. So we split.

When it was time to register for the spring semester, the athletic department wanted me to sign up for all the snap physical education courses, but I refused. I wasn't taking the Mickey Mouse route. I'd rather flunk out in the good courses than get good grades in the snap courses that don't do you any good. So I signed up for the courses that would lead me toward my degree.

I stayed in school and upset the odds by getting my degree, something some of my Duke teammates weren't able to do, or didn't do for one reason or another. Throughout my college career I carried the stigma of those lousy freshman grades. I went to summer school every year, even though I hated it and it deprived me of the opportunity to earn some money and have fun with my friends. Summer school was important, because it meant I wouldn't have to carry a heavy load in the fall. I never dated and I never went out to dinner. That way I was able to save money and devote my attention to school instead of night life.

My sophomore year was the best I had at Duke. We had a good team, good enough to get invited to the Gator Bowl, but we turned it down because we were all tired of football by that time. That's another subject—bowl games—but more about that later.

I regret to report that I got another F the first semester of my sophomore year—in statistics. It was then I decided to change my major from business to history. My decision was ratified the following semester. I made the dean's list, which pulled me out of the disaster area.

On the football field we won everything, and I played both ways—fullback on offense and middle linebacker on defense. The only negative note on the whole year—aside from that F in statistics—was a knee injury in spring practice that made me miss most of the action. But I came back in time for the intrasquad game, and again that burning aggressiveness came to the surface.

Our team lost and I was so incensed that I wouldn't even walk up to the other team. Even though we were all Duke players, that didn't make any difference. Practice or not, teammates or not, I was sore as hell because my team lost.

At the start of my junior year I really expected to make

All-American as a fullback—assuming all went well. A lot of people at Duke were talking about it, some of the local writers were predicting it and every once in a while one of the coaches would bring up the subject.

Then, as these things so often happen, fate dived in. It came in the form of a fourth-string clown on my own team. We were having a scrimmage and I rammed into the middle of the line while carrying the ball, and a big pileup followed. After the play was over, this clown came in and dived on top of me from the rear after I had relaxed my legs. He twisted my left knee, and that complicated things for a long time.

I rested the knee because I didn't want anyone fooling around with it. We had two weeks before our first game against South Carolina, but I didn't practice. I got ready for the game by taping my knee heavily. I played both offense and defense in the opener, but it was on defense that it happened. As I was running toward the ball carrier, a South Carolina player hit me from the left, and the same knee got it again. At halftime I retaped the knee after placing a piece of sponge rubber against it. That made it feel better. I played the rest of the game, and I think I scored two touchdowns, kicked two extra points and wound up doing all the scoring for Duke.

The consensus was: What the hell, if that's what he can do when he's hurt, think of what he can do when he's healthy. Still, I didn't think I played that well—the touchdowns were just short yardage plays.

But the frustrations started to pile up. A few weeks later I hurt my left knee again, against North Carolina State. By now it was clear that I would not make All-American, certainly not that season. Nothing seemed to be going right. My knee injury not only bothered me physically but weighed heavily on my mind as well. I lost a lot of weight and developed an ulcer—all this while I'm hitting the books and trying to complete my college education.

The frustrations hit such a level that I even had a blow-up with my head coach, Bill Murray. I was practicing field goals just before the start of our game against Georgia Tech when Murray came over to tell me how to kick. I told him I was kicking the same way I always did. He said, "You'll kick the way I want you to."

I got sore and said, "I'll kick the goddam ball the way I want to kick it, and don't you come around and tell me anything different." We had a big argument right there on the field. Now I was teed off at everyone.

To add to my discontent, our first-string quarterback, a knowledgeable leader named Dave Uible, got hurt. He was replaced by a guy named Scotty Glacken, who was not one of my favorite persons. Glacken always seemed too cocky and loud to me, and, and I just don't like people like that. This only added to the burden of what was becoming a wearying and deeply disappointing season.

Well, the supreme irony came in our game against Georgia Tech. I was blocking—for Scotty Glacken, of all people—when my right knee got in the way of two Tech defensive tackles. That sealed the season for me.

It was almost a relief for me, because of all the problems and frustrations. But that knee injury—my fourth—was the worst pain I had ever felt. A few years later, when I was with the Colts, I hurt my left knee again and had to have it operated on, but it never hurt half as much as when I got it in that Tech game.

After I got hurt, one of the Tech players was screaming,

"I got you, Curtis. I got you, you hot dog." And I thought: "What the hell kind of business is this? You hurt a guy on purpose? And then brag about it?" In the same game, one of our assistant coaches wanted me to hurt one of the Tech guys who had knee trouble. I told him I didn't give a damn whether he wanted me to or not, I wouldn't do it then and never would.

The Tech game injury didn't require an operation. They just put a cast on the knee to keep it tight. I didn't go to practice, and this bothered some of the assistant coaches, who somehow figured I wasn't being gung-ho enough, or something stupid like that. And Scotty Glacken, that great Duke quarterback, came to me and told me the team didn't need me and would win without me. After that they played about .500 ball. I don't think my absence hurt them as much as Glacken's presence.

They took the cast off in two weeks, and I started to run a little, but it was obvious that I still had a bad right knee. Some of the coaches continued to bug me and demanded to know when I would be ready to play again, and I told them I wasn't going to play any more that season. Just before our last game, against North Carolina, they really put the pressure on to get me in that lineup. But I never got that excited about beating Carolina anyhow. To me they were just another team. We lost the game, and that was the end of the season for all of us.

Spring came and I got myself organized in preparation for what would be my senior year. It was an unorthodox practice period, to say the least. For one thing, I took the daily precaution of taping my legs from my ankles to the middle of my thighs—which meant I had to keep my legs shaved throughout the practice period. Second, there was some unfinished business to attend to. I made up a list of teammates I had scores to settle with—those who had joined Glacken in bad-mouthing me, and those who had upset me for other reasons, like bullying some of their own teammates in practice just to impress the coaches.

I made sure I got even with every name on that list. It was my spring of satisfaction. My run-in with Chuck Stavins was typical of the way I went about things that spring. Stavins was always picking on one of our tackles, Don Lynch. Lynch never would say anything, even though he was big enough to take care of himself. It seemed that Stavins was just bristling to get into a fight with Lynch. Mr. Stavins therefore was on my list of guys to get even with.

In a scrimmage I lined up opposite Stavins, who was an offensive tackle. I was playing middle linebacker. I said, "Listen, Stavins, today I'm putting you down for treating Lynch the way you do. You will not say anything else to Lynch." The play started and I went right for Stavins and pounded him into the ground. The play swept away from us, but I made no attempt to go for the ball carrier. I just stayed there on the ground with Stavins, beating the living hell out of him. I didn't let him up until I told him if he ever bothered Lynch again, he'd get it again, only worse. He outweighed me by twenty pounds, but he knew I would do it again without any hesitation at all. Don Lynch was never bothered again by Mr. Stavins.

I shook up Glacken a couple of times, too, with a couple of extra rough tackles in scrimmages. Once he jumped up and threw the ball at me. I grabbed him by the shirt and told him I'd snap his head right off if he ever did that again. He never did.

50

So I was causing a lot of trouble, but I was settling a lot of scores. After that I had a good spring and performed well. The running game looked promising, because I was running with Jay Calabrese, the number two fullback, behind me. We were both having a good spring. Jay had been a teammate of Scotty Glacken's at St. John's High in Washington, but I hit it off much better with Jay. He's still a good friend of mine.

When the 1964 season opened, I didn't think about making All-American or getting signed by the pros or anything else. I concentrated on playing well and staying healthy. I decided not to tape my knees, just to see how well healed they were. They were fine. We played South Carolina in our opener and lost by two points, as I recall. One of our coaches, Doug Knotts, told me after the game that one of the South Carolina coaches had said I played the best game ever played in that South Carolina stadium by a linebacker.

It turned out to be only a so-so season. We lost to Georgia Tech and Tulane, plus a couple of others. Against North Carolina I played as hard as I could, because the game was supposed to be a match between me and Carolina's Ken Willard, now of the San Francisco 49-ers. I was having a good game and then, naturally, I got hurt. I dislocated my shoulder. Fortunately, it was the last game of the season, and on that note I ended my college football career.

By this time I had heard I was going to be drafted by the pros, probably the Chicago Bears. One of their representatives told me Detroit was also interested in me and that I would probably go in one of the top rounds of the draft by the NFL teams. In the AFL, the Kansas City

Chiefs and the San Diego Chargers were also interested in me, but I always wanted to play in the NFL because that was really pro football to me, with the best teams and the most prestige. I was surprised that the pros were as interested in me as they were. I wasn't all that sure I was worth it, but I wasn't going to discourage anyone.

I found myself in a tug-of-war, and I was the rope. A guy named Joe Tereshinski, a former Redskin, was representing the NFL, while Ted Youngling, one of the assistant coaches at Duke and a guy I once had a run-in with, was the agent following me around for the AFL. The two leagues were still competing in those days for signing their draft choices, and during the drafting they stayed glued to the college players who figured to get picked.

We were all holed up at the Washingtonian Motel in Maryland between my home in Rockville and Gaithersburg. The NFL had put me in a room there to make sure they had instant access to my signature on a contract the minute I was drafted. But Youngling was in the same hotel, stalking me every step for the AFL. We wanted to watch the draft on TV, Dad and me, but Tereshinski turned it off. They almost lost me there when that happened, because I didn't like that or the way Tereshinski was talking to my Dad.

The draft was scheduled for the next day, and Tereshinski took me for a long ride the night before, trying to shake Youngling from our trail. We sped out the motel driveway and across Interstate Route 70S and started to head for some country roads. Youngling spotted us leaving and stayed hot on our trail. Then we darted off the road and hid behind a house, and he went speeding past us on down the road.

We came back to the road and went to a private country club where Youngling couldn't get in. I thought the whole thing was funny as hell.

I was picked number one by the Colts and number three by the Chiefs. The Chiefs tried to get hold of me by having some girl call up and identify herself as my fiancé. I didn't have a fiancé. The Colts asked me how much money I wanted to sign with them instead of with the Chiefs and, hell, I didn't really know. So I said I thought about $15,000. They said, "Okay, we'll give you fifteen this year and seventeen next year." (Shoot, when I said fifteen, I meant for two years.) Then they said, "We'll also give you a bonus of $22,000 for signing." So instead of 15,000, I was coming up with a two-year total of 54,000. Right away I was beginning to like pro football.

As the years went by I learned that signing with the Colts was the best thing I could have done. I'm in my eighth year with them now. They're the most winning team in football. We went to the old Runner-up Bowl in my rookie season and again in my second year. We played in the Super Bowl after the 1968 season and again after 1970. I've just been lucky as hell, and the avenues are getting wider all the time—broken thumb or no broken thumb.

Damned if that old thumb didn't come around sooner than I expected. I knew right after practice that I would be ready for the game against the Buffalo Bills. Although it hurt like hell, I just made up my mind I had to get used to it and get back into the lineup, so I started hitting at the beginning of practice and kept it up. I could feel the pins in my thumb stinging clean through the skin.

I decided to hit hard to test my effectiveness to the fullest and also to take my mind off the injury, and it worked. I told our linebacker coach, Hank Bullough, "I'll be ready. If I'm playing poorly or if we're winning easily, you can take me out. But I'll be able to play."

The one thing I feared about the upcoming game was half time. I've never liked the interruption of half time. I'd play four quarters in a row if they let me. The only thing half time does to me is slow me down. Now there was the distinct possibility of my cooling off physically and psychologically, with more time to think about my injury, and that would do me no good. I really dreaded that half time. Here's how I mapped my thumb strategy: I would play with my fingers covered completely with tape, so they wouldn't snap straight back toward my wrist because of the cast. I'd wear a plaster of Paris tip over the exposed portion of the thumb. I'd be taped like a mummy from my fingernails up to my elbow, thus keeping within the specifications spelled out in the league rules. The cast would be reinforced with a lot of cotton. Now all I had to do was figure out how to keep my fingers crossed.

Buffalo had a good offense, with a big line and O. J. Simpson running behind it. It would be interesting to see if they tried to pick on me because of my injury. I was fair game and that was a fair trick to try. But it would make me angry and I'd play that much better.

The Colts weren't taking any chances. We had five to

seven pages of assignments for each blitz, and ten pages for each pass defense.

Rick Volk provided the comic relief, as he so often does, during the week's practice. As usual, it was all unintentional. He showed up in his 1935 Rolls Royce and was dressed in clothes from the same era. He was wearing two-toned wing-tip shoes, gray plaid knickers, gray knee socks, a white turtleneck sweater. All he lacked were a scarf and goggles and the white snap-down cap. He tried to sneak into the dressing room when he thought we would all be out on the field. But we were all still there. So he really got a royal reception.

Rick's the kind of guy who is an easy target. Every team has one, and sometimes those guys lead with their chins and invite the ribbing that comes from their teammates. Like the time Rick showed up late for practice and somebody asked, "Did your wife make you do the dishes today?"

Rick said, "No, I didn't have to do the dishes today."

About ten guys hollered back, "What do you mean today?"

So Rick fumbles all over himself and stammers out an explanation that he didn't mean to say today, that he really doesn't have to do the dishes at his house any day and that's not what he meant to say and on and on and on.

Don McCafferty finally put an end to it. He just said quietly, "That will cost you twenty-five dollars, Rick, for being late."

Chapter 4

I survived the game against Buffalo—including half time. And I was able to play the whole game. I got lucky and intercepted two passes and made eleven unassisted tackles. The Associated Press voted me the Defensive Player of the Week.

We simply clobbered the daylights out of the Bills, 43–0. It was significant to me that, with that kind of lopsided score, the headline in the *Washington Post* read:

DEFENSIVE DISPLAY LIFTS COLTS, 43–0

Even when we score 43 points, our defense was conspicuous. No wonder, when you look at the game closely.

Buffalo gained a total of 4 yards on the ground, and only 121 yards in the air. O. J. Simpson carried seven times and wound up with minus 10 yards. He caught two short passes for only 14 yards. We intercepted four passes and we sacked their quarterbacks nine times—nine times—for 76 yards.

Dennis Shaw completed only two of nine passes for 30 yards before being lifted. My first interception was on only his second pass of the game. I grabbed it at the Buffalo 32-yard line and returned it to the one, after feeling like a fullback again for 31 yards. Norm Bulaich got the touchdown for us. (If I had been able to go all the way, two things I would not have done: I would not have "spiked" the ball, jamming it into the turf, and I would not have slapped the other guys' open hands with a "gimme five" gesture. I'm the old-fashioned type. When you score a touchdown in football or hit a home run in baseball, I prefer the simple handshake. Anything else is hot-dog stuff in my opinion.)

After the game O. J. Simpson paid our defense some nice tributes, saying we were better than the Minnesota Vikings, who had earlier beat the Bills, 19–0. Simpson said the Vikings had "a very slight edge" in their Front Four, "but the Colts have such fine linebackers they've got it all over the Vikings. We couldn't pass on either one of these teams, but we couldn't run a bit on the Colts. That's because their linebackers fill up the holes so well when they're there. Overall, the Colts play more as a unit, whereas the Vikings rely very heavily on that Front Four."

Bubba Smith was needling O. J. as the post-game conversation went on. They're old buddies, and O. J. was saying he had one success in the game: He threw a block on Bubba that put him out for a couple of series of plays. So when they're talking about it in the Bills' dressing room after the game, Bubba says, "I don't want to hear about it. We squeezed you today, Orange Juice."

O. J. couldn't get mad at Bubba. Nobody can. He's six feet, eight inches tall and weighs 270 pounds and he's everybody's pal. I call him King and I tell him it's because he looks like King Kong. I keep telling him to go shinny up the Empire State Building and he calls me honky and I call him nigger and we both laugh like hell about it.

To make it a perfect day, I even got a game ball by vote of the other players. Tom Mitchell, our good receiver, got one, too. I'm not real sure I deserved either the ball or the A.P honor. I didn't do all that well on the running plays, because I was not tackling well. I was favoring my arm and I had to force myself to play with abandon and forget that thumb and the cast. The thumb really hurt a few times when I fell on it, especially when I got tackled after the two interceptions. And once, when I grabbed O. J. Simpson with my right hand, I thought that thumb was going to drop right off.

A lot of the guys had advised me not to play. Their reasoning was: We shouldn't have any trouble with Buffalo, so why endure a lot of pain if you don't have to? There were several reasons. One was that Ray May was doing well in my place, having moved over from his spot on the outside, and I didn't want any doubt as to just who the hell the Colts' middle linebacker is. For another reason, the team seemed to be ready for the game and I wanted to be part of what I hoped would be an impressive victory. And maybe most of all, I just could not allow a small broken bone in my thumb to cause me to miss two or three or four games. I had missed one already, and that was enough.

Before the game one of the officials came over to check my cast and told me to be careful because if I hit anybody with that thing he'd have to give me fifteen yards. I told him not to worry, I wasn't going to make any more contact with that cast than I had to, and I sure as hell wasn't going to go around looking for somebody to swing it at.

On Buffalo's first offensive play of the game, I was very aware of this stupid thumb. The guard came up and tripped me, and the tight end came down and tried to hit me, too. I got up and tried to get over to the play on the right side. Ted Hendricks made the play, so I wasn't needed there. But I felt stupid because I had fallen down, and I hurt because I had hit my thumb in the fall. But another run and a pass got them nothing, so we came off the field, and I had survived my first series of plays with a broken thumb and a mummy's cast.

On the next series the Bills tried another sweep and I was able to get to the play and help out, even though the cast was beginning to weigh on me. It's a damn heavy thing to have to carry around and tackle people with.

On the next play, when Dennis Shaw dropped back to pass, I also dropped back to protect my part of our defensive zone. I saw him glance to one side and I lit out toward that spot, and sure enough that's where he threw it. I cradled the ball into my midsection, right in front of Ted Hendricks, who would have intercepted it himself if I hadn't got there first. I saw a lot of tacklers come from my left, so I decided to cut back and go against the grain. After 30 yards I got hit. I spun around trying to break the tackle and cushion my fall, but I landed on the ball, which was in my right hand, and it nearly killed me. I remember getting up from that play and thinking, "My God, what the hell am I doing this for? What kind of way is this to make a living?"

Now I was getting more confident. In the second quarter the Bills ran a play they call the fifteen straight, a play over their right tackle to our right and over our right guard. I hit the tackle and he came down on me, but I tried to play around him with my left hand and not use my right. He pushed me back a little. Another guy hit me, then a third. I got around all three of them eventually, but if the ballcarrier had been coming at me, he would have been able to pick up five yards. However, the other guys were doing so well working together that the Bills lost three yards on the play. Maybe the fact that Buffalo used three guys on me was one reason.

In the same quarter Shaw threw another pass that hooked to the tight end—the same play as before. When I drop back on a pass play, I look quickly to both sides to make sure I know what's unfolding anywhere in my territory, but I also keep an eye on the quarterback. Just as he did the first time, Shaw gave the play away. Again he was looking where he was going to throw the ball instead of using some fakes. Experienced quarterbacks look to the left and the right and line up a number of receivers. But this will come in time to Shaw. He's a first-rate prospect as a quarterback and as a passer.

I ran over to where I had seen Shaw look and this time

60

I caught the ball in my left arm, thank goodness. I started running, but several Buffalo tacklers caught up with me. I got only seven yards on the return, but I was feeling great now.

I even got through the half time with no real problems, mainly because after those first two periods my confidence came back and I didn't really think I had anything to worry about. My main problem was that I was tired, awfully tired. I had been awake almost all night worrying about the game. But I wasn't about to take any pep pills. Despite what Dave Meggyesy says, football players are not a bunch of hopped-up dope addicts. I don't take any of that stuff. It tires you out and makes you weak. And even if you're hopped up, you're only fooling yourself. You may think you're playing better but you're not. Your reaction time is slower, and chances are you'll play worse than if you hadn't taken anything.

Let's talk about this dope question for a minute while we're at it. Football's critics have their own clichés for that, too—terms like "widespread use" and "on the rise" (whatever that's supposed to indicate). You hear a lot of misinformation about players taking bennies, for example. I, for one, don't take them. A lot of other players don't take them, either. Consider those who do—and not just football players. People on diets take these pills daily. People with allergies take them two, three or four times a day. Truck drivers swallow them like candy. And all this pill consumption has been going on for years; and nobody has written any books about the "widespread use" of these pills among America's dieting women or about such pills being "on the rise" among America's allergy patients. So why point to football players? Especially when those who do take them take one pill a week? A football player who takes a diet pill as his pep pill does so on the day of the game. If his team goes all the way to the Super Bowl and if he has taken them from the beginning of the exhibition season, he will have taken twenty-three pills over a period of five months. Over that same duration an allergy victim, for example, if he takes only one pill a day will have taken 150 pills—and maybe also get a shot in his arm once a week, so that's twenty shots. But no one seriously believes that allergy victims or truck drivers or weight-reducers are dope addicts.

These are diet pills we're talking about. Not hard drugs like LSD or even marijuana. If you had trouble getting to sleep last night and took a sleeping pill, would that make you a dope addict?

Meggyesy, in an angling sort of way, says some players take pills for practice. I question that. Only one player ever did that for the Colts and that was some years ago. He couldn't make the grade, with or without the pills, and he was cut. I've never seen anyone else take a pill during the week. The only thing I depend on is adrenalin, and I don't need a pill for that. I just get myself psyched up before a game and that gets me pepped up plenty, even if I haven't had enough sleep. Anyway, that's what I did before the Bills game. Obviously it worked.

We prepped for the Giants game during World Series week. That seems to be the one time of the year when everyone is a baseball fan.

Speaking of baseball, I recently made the mistake of reading *Ball Four*, Jim Bouton's book. It was awful. I hope he enjoys every one of the dollars he makes off that piece of trash. He never was much pitcher except when the Yankees were winning for every hurler who walked out to the mound. Bouton hasn't been a big winner since 1964. Lord, that's almost a decade ago. No wonder he decided to write a book.

The stuff that Bouton writes about with such drooling delight goes on everywhere—in sports, in business, in government. Hell, it almost brought about the collapse of the whole damn government in England about ten years ago. In any group you've got guys who are cheating on their wives and some who aren't, some who go out and get drunk and some who don't.

You read about a minister running off with the organist, but that doesn't mean all ministers do it. Some lawyers are convicted of cheating their clients, but do all lawyers do it? If a teacher totals his car while loaded on Saturday night, are all teachers drunkards and bad drivers? No reasonable person would feel that way about any of these groups, or about any other group, despite the occasional bad apple or the occasional bad publicity. Why feel that way about all pro athletes because of a few malcontents who couldn't make the grade and aren't even in the game any more?

When a trashy book about ballplayers comes out, kids read it and they think this is the way to act. They grow up thinking that way. A lot of those kids, even if they aren't influenced in the wrong direction, are at least disappointed and disillusioned by what they read about their heroes, so it hurts kids in two ways. That's the real harm about books like that. It hurts kids. Nice going, Bouton.

Prepping for the game against the Giants was sheer brutality—and all because of Fran Tarkenton. He may be a friend of mine, but he sure does make me work a lot harder before I play against him. With all that scrambling he does he can beat you, and he sure was doing more than ever last year because of the Giants' injury-ridden offensive line. So Fran had to play it by ear and hope for the best.

The Giants use a lot of formations, and our offense must have run every one of them against us in practice. Karl Douglas, our black quarterback, was playing Tarkenton's role, wearing number 10 and scrambling all over the field.

I happened to be in a fog that week. It was the first time I had to think about what I was doing in I don't know how long. Everything had always been basic to me, but now there were many adjustments to take care of Tarkenton—including even a double checkoff. For example: If we spotted something just before the Giants started their play, and they adjusted, we then adjusted to their adjustment. I don't know how much more physical this game is becoming, as some people say, but it's one hell of a lot more mental.

Zone defenses, which the Colts have used for several years and which other teams are beginning to put in, make life much more complicated for everyone. You can't just play man-to-man, with each defender concentrating on one offensive man. You have a zone to defend and you

What could Coach Don MaCafferty be thinking? Maybe. "The game plan, fellahs, the game plan." (*Ronald Ross*)

Earl Morrall is a good listener, but some fans worry that his arm may not have that old zing (*Ronald Ross*).

Although John Unitas still looks pretty classy fading back to pass, most experts believe the Old Pro's seasons are numbered (*Ronald Ross*).

Mike Curtis is the stalwart, combat-ready man in the middle of the Baltimore Colts' outstanding defense (*Ronald Ross*).

Getting hit by Bubba Smith is as devastating as picking up
Bubba's lunch tab (*Ronald Ross*).

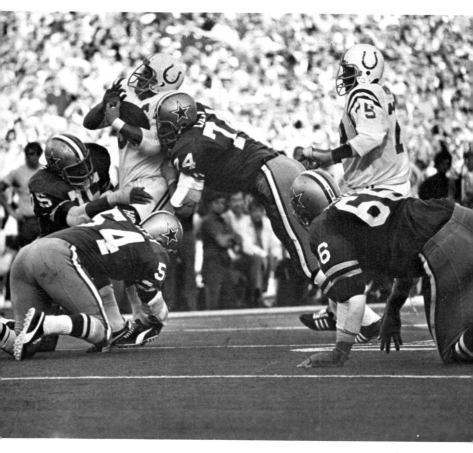

A trio of Dallas Cowboys—Jethro Pugh (75), Bob Lilly (74) and Chuck Howley (54)—gang-tackle Mike Curtis following his interception late in the quarter of the 1971 Super Bowl game. The interception set up a winning field goal in the final seconds of the game. (*Wide World Photos*)

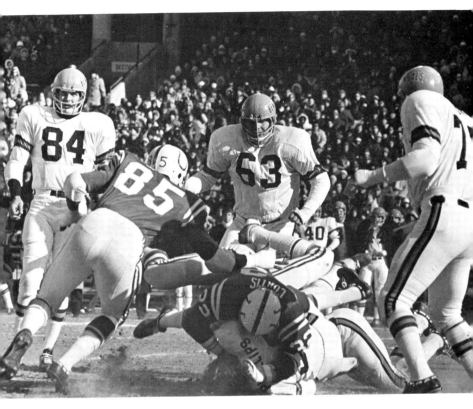

One difference between God's green earth and artificial turf is
demonstrated by Mike Curtis as he grinds Cincinnati Bengals'
Jess Phillips' head into real dirt (*Wide World Photos*).

Line Judge Bill Schleibaum moves in to break up a fight as Mike Curtis and Boston Patriots' Tom Beer wrestle each other to the ground (*Wide World Photos*).

have to know who's coming into your zone and how to react. This depends on the game situation, the ability of the other team, the quarterback's ability to read the defense, and his knowing whether to check off at the line of scrimmage with an audible signal while calling a different play at the same time. Successful zone defense also depends on the knowledge and ability of the ten other men in the huddle to pick up the check-off and the audible for the new play—and on and on and on. If you think you're confused, how do you think we feel? And you're supposed to digest and assimilate all these things in two or three seconds.

If only it weren't so complicated. After all, it's only a game. Why should it be this way? I like to keep things simple. I wish you could just go out there and tackle and be tackled and run and pass and see whether your team is better than the other team. That's what this game is all about, isn't it? But people complicate everything these days, even games.

Chapter 5

New York—how I hate that place. Every time I go there I hate it more.

Too damn many people, for one thing. I can't believe man was meant to live like that, everybody jammed together and getting angry with one another because of the tensions created by the crowded conditions. And no trees. And all that pollution and traffic.

It seems to me that about eighty per cent of the New Yorkers I meet are obnoxious as hell, completely lacking in courtesy and basic human kindness. I don't tip cab drivers in any city, because I resent the way they expect it and demand it, and when I come to New York and don't tip them they give me a lot of guff. It happens every trip. Sometimes I finally tell them to step outside if they don't like it, but they never do. They just have their big mouths.

They are not alone, though. They just seem to reflect the attitude of most of the people you run into up there. Los Angeles is the same way. And they live a lot worse than the rest of us, yet they look down their noses at us, as if we're all a bunch of hayseeds because we don't live in New York or Los Angeles. When I go into New York, I just gird my loins for the worst.

They talk about those Yankee Stadium crowds and their effect on the visiting teams, as if the visitors are really unlucky to have to beat the Giants. Hell, I'll tell you something about those Yankee Stadium crowds. They make me play twice as hard. All I have to do is picture the average New Yorker and I want to kill the Giants. I just hate the city and the people so much I want to take it out on the team. If they were nice people they wouldn't bother me so much, and maybe I wouldn't play so hard against the Giants. But with these rude, crude, hostile New Yorkers helping out, it's never hard to get up for a game against the Giants or the Jets on their own turf.

At least the fans in New York don't have ready access to us the way they have in Buffalo and used to have in Boston. In Buffalo the Bills play in a small, cozy stadium, with the seats close to the field—too close. The Bills always seem to be losing, so the fans compensate by throwing insults and snowballs at the other team's players on the bench. In 1970 Roy Jefferson got so fed up with the Buffalo fans' conduct he went after them. Fortunately for everyone, he didn't make it into the stands—but he was headed that way, with fire in his eye. I guess the fire helped melt the snowball.

In Boston—very proper Boston—the Patriots played their home games at Harvard's field until moving into their new stadium at Foxboro last year. Up there those high-born Boston kids used to sneak up behind our bench and steal our footballs. The police would just stand around and watch them. They seemed afraid to get involved. I don't know what the crime rate is in Boston, but they must lead the FBI statistics in the stolen-football category.

The Miami fans are the most avid, the loudest in their cheering for the old home team. No wonder. In Miami it's easy. They have a great team and a great coach and they're winners. But it's to their credit that the fans conduct themselves in a decent way, accentuating the positive things and refraining from the insults and the boos just because the other players wear a different kind of uniform. In my experience Dallas fans have been just about as well-behaved. Those Southwest people know their football and appreciate it and show no need to get personal in their treatment of visiting players.

The best fans, in my opinion, are in Washington, and I don't say that because I'm from the Washington suburbs. They come to those games in coat and tie and cheer like mad for the Redskins, who have given them nothing but losers for twenty-five years, except for 1969 under Vince Lombardi and last year under George Allen. They are cordial to opposing players and they don't throw debris onto the field or yell a lot of personal insults. They're well-behaved fans who prove you can go to a ball game, cheer your lungs out and still behave yourself. I like that, and that's why I enjoy playing in front of the Washington fans.

Also, there's always a slew of celebrities on hand in Robert F. Kennedy Stadium—senators, congressmen, members of the Cabinet—people who are hardly animals or rednecks. And they're not caught "in a sexual frenzy," as Meggyesy claims. They just like football. That doesn't mean they're like Roman emperors turning thumbs down and sentencing the Christians to the lions.

In New York, Jacqueline Kennedy Onassis and Caroline and John Jr. came out to root for the old home team. Not to witness the dehumanization of two groups of grown men, not to engage in the decaying of the moral fiber of American society, not to do anything that the amateur psychiatrists read into the sport of football. They were just there to have a good time. What was so awful about that? Ed Sullivan was there, too, and the wife of Astronaut Scott Carpenter, and Gordon MacRae, the singer, and a lot of other celebs. Too bad most New York fans are not as nice.

The rest of the team must feel the same way about New York fans. We beat the Giants, 31–7, and, as United Press International said, it was a rout. Bulaich scored twice, once on an incredible sideline run of 34 yards and once on a 27-yard pass from Earl Morrall. Earl threw three touchdown passes, and I know it was a sweet day for him, because he used to play for the Giants and he was extremely unhappy when the Giants gave him the cold shoulder after they got Tarkenton. He was a Giant in uniform only. So in this game he was a star—for the Colts.

Frankly, I didn't think we played all that well—the

defense allowed 260 yards—but the papers said we looked great. I was disappointed in my game because I didn't seem to be hitting as well as I should and I wasn't reacting well. I felt slow and sluggish. The cast was still bothering me and I couldn't seem to use my right arm to tackle. It's pretty hard to get hold of someone without your thumb.

I was doubly disappointed because of my so-so performance in the presence of those New York writers. Those guys can do a lot for a player's professional reputation, and that's what a player relies on for advancement, like any other employee. New York is still the sports publicity capital of the world, and when I play there I'm always aware that my performance will be judged by those writers. And that judgment will be reported by the wire services, the radio and TV networks, the influential *New York Times* and the national sports magazines. It's nice to win, but how you look while you're winning means something, too. Especially when you're playing in New York.

One clue that I wasn't hitting as much became apparent at practice. I looked at my helmet and noticed it didn't have any marks on it and I said something about it out loud. Freddie Miller heard it and said, "Yeah. Look at mine. It's got a lot of marks. You've got to start hitting, Curtis."

After the game I was talking to Fran Tarkenton in our dressing room and I was kidding him about running a quarterback sneak for a first down on fourth and inches early in the game. I said, "What the hell are you doing calling a play like that in that situation?"

He threw back his head and laughed and said, "Well,

when you've got the sixteenth best yard-gainer in the league in your backfield, you call on him—and that's who I am." (Incidentally, he made the first down, with inches to spare.)

People wonder why the Giants have fallen on hard times after so many winning seasons. The answer comes in two words: No material. It's a result of poor recruiting, and it means, in my opinion, the top man is at fault. That's Wellington Mara,—he's the guy you have to blame in such a situation. It all goes back to the top. If the owner is on the ball, his abilities are reflected by the entire organization.

As for head coach Alex Webster, he just hasn't proved himself. His team showed some improvement in 1970, but last year the Giants were stumbling along all over again.

Their running backs are a good example of what ails the Giants. Tucker Frederickson was great, but that was before he had his knees carved up in surgery. In 1971 he ran in slow motion. Everyone talks about how good Ron Johnson is, and I agree. He has to be great, because all you have to do to stop the Giants' running game is key on Johnson. He still gains yardage, however. It's amazing he gains anything at all the way the defenses are able to zero in on him. And there's nothing else on offense, except Fran Tarkenton, whose scrambling exposes their lack of offense, a deficiency matched by their lack of defense.

No material.

Everyone seemed to be working more conscientiously, studying his assignments harder, taking game films home after practice and in general showing a serious attitude for our next game—against the Vikings. We knew we would have to hit hard to beat Minnesota. One good thing about playing the Vikings as far as the defensive team is concerned is that they keep to simple offensive formations, such as straight power plays, medium sweeps about five yards outside the end and standard pass plays. No razzmatazz. They just try to blow you out. They have good backs and good receivers, but only an average offensive line. I think their defensive line is their whole team, with Alan Page alone about half of it.

They play good basic football. They don't try to do a whole lot of different things. They just do what they have to and they do it well.

When you beat Minnesota, you have a hell of a team. When you lose to them, you might still have a good team. But when the Vikings beat you by a high score, you have problems. They usually nickel-and-dime you to death with fourteen or sixteen points a game, and they are likely to beat you by two points or on a last-minute field goal. They seem to lead the league in games won by less than one touchdown.

Win or lose, we would have to battle hard to beat Miami for our division championship. Even after the Vikings, we faced some toughies, like the Rams and Oakland. But if we could beat Minnesota we'd feel pretty confident about going on to the Super Bowl.

Speaking of the Super Bowl, I still get asked often—too often—how the Jets ever managed to beat us following the 1968 season. My memory of that Super Bowl is that the whole thing seemed like a big carnival. We had a hotel on the beach north of Miami, and the players brought their wives and their children along for the entire week.

So right away it was a party atmosphere, and kids were running all over the joint and wives were coming up and getting money from their husbands and going shopping while the players baby-sat with the kids. Some of the wives spent a thousand dollars on clothes while we were there. I was glad I was single.

We had to travel an hour to get to our practice field. And an hour to get back. There were a million reporters hanging around. You could never rest. They were always phoning your room and stalking you wherever you went. There was never any time to relax or even to think about the game.

Through it all, of course, we thought for sure we would win, and I felt the same way. I didn't have much respect for the Jets. I figured simply that something would happen to make us win. Our practices were good all week, so everyone was having fun. But when the game rolled around, the players seemed sluggish.

I didn't start to worry about it until Earl Morrall missed Jimmy Orr in the end zone. There was nobody within twenty-five yards of Jimmy. But Earl threw it to Jerry Hill instead and it was intercepted. Then he threw to Tom Mitchell and it bounced off his pads for an interception on what would have been a touchdown. So instead of two touchdowns for the Colts, it became two interceptions for the Jets. Then we started to press.

At the half we were losing and I was so teed off I went into the shower room and just sat there and wanted to hide. But Don Shula found me and said, "You'd better get back over there with the rest of the defense. We've got to do something in the second half."

What frustrated me even more was that the Jets weren't

running anything my way. Then they threw a pass in my territory and I made a mistake. I was so anxious to hit Namath I blitzed without even thinking of the back coming through the middle. It was Emerson Boozer, and he was supposed to be my man. I forgot all about him and headed straight for Namath, who hit Boozer for five or six yards.

The second half was not a bit better than the first. The outcome was that 16–7 stunner, the Jets scoring one of the biggest upsets in pro football history. They beat us soundly, no question about that. I saw a picture in the paper the next day of Don Shinnick, one of our linebackers, congratulating Namath. But I wasn't congratulating anyone. Carroll Rosenbloom, our owner, had planned a big party for the team and he still held it. I went, against my wishes, picked up two bottles of champagne and went off into a corner by myself and said to hell with the world.

I didn't worry about avenging that defeat, not right away anyhow. I just wanted to forget about it. I was crushed by it. The dressing room was just dead after the game, a real morgue. I hid from the reporters by ducking into the john. That's where I got undressed. Then the reporters finally caught up with me and one of them asked a couple of exceedingly stupid questions, not sensitive just dumb, but I had to put up with it anyhow.

Our team was twice as good as the Jets. Twice as good. There just wasn't any comparison between the two teams. If Orr and Mitchell had been able to catch those two passes for touchdowns early in the game, it would have been a romp. We've beaten them every time we've played them since. That says something. But it still can't erase that day in the Super Bowl.

We couldn't get up for them, that's all. Can you imagine not being able to get up for the championship game? If we had been up for that game the way we were for every other game that year we would have beaten the hell out of them. You'd think that, being pros, we would be able to get up for any "must" game, especially the championship, with the winning team winding up with $25,000 a man, but it wasn't so that day.

In Super Bowl V following the 1970 season, things were different, and the result was better. To begin with, the wives weren't with us. It wasn't a family picnic. We weren't bothered as much by reporters, because they thought we had played an easy schedule and maybe weren't so great. And we were miles and miles from the beach, but our practice field was only ten minutes away. Everything was just the opposite from the Super Bowl of two years earlier, including our attitude.

Still, we would have lost the second game if not for some breaks. One of them, strangely enough, involved an injury to John Unitas. He got racked up by Jethro Pugh, and Earl Morrall had to come in. John had not been completing his passes, but Morrall got the job done, with the help of Mel Renfro's fingers. After he hit John Mackey on a critical pass that tipped Renfro's fingers, we were able to drive in for a key score.

So we were lucky at that. Our defense forced enough fumbles and interceptions and that made the difference. I was glad to win it and ease some of the pain from Super Bowl III, but I wanted to win big. We didn't.

In fact, we were only tied with about fifty seconds left when Craig Morton tried a pass and I intercepted it and got the ball back close enough for a field goal attempt by Jim O'Brien. I've been asked many times since if I was surprised that Morton decided to throw, and my answer is always no. We had a tie game at that point. I figured they would try to win it right there, instead of gambling on a sudden-death win. The pass was just over Dan Reeves' fingers into my hands.

O'Brien got us the field goal and we were the world champions.

Only I didn't feel like it. We were just lucky. Unlucky in January, 1969, and lucky in January, 1971. Maybe things do even out after all. But I wanted us to win like champions and we didn't. I just wanted to get out of Miami after that.

In the 1969 season we had our ups and downs, and we were never in the running. But in 1970, even in training camp, aware of our easier schedule, I was determined we would get into the Super Bowl again and win it this time. I would not accept anything else. The papers noted toward the end of that season that if we hadn't had such an easy schedule we would never have made it. We beat teams like San Diego and Houston by a handful of points. But then maybe we would have played a lot harder against more respectable teams.

Chapter 6

Well, we dominated the Vikings. More than I could have expected. We had sixteen first downs to their nine. We had 276 total yards to their 153. We ran seventy-one offensive plays to their forty-seven. We completed nineteen passes to their seven.

And we lost.

Our offense was totally inept at one of the most important aspects of the game—scoring points. We managed a field goal by Jim O'Brien and that was it. We dominated them so much that we still had a shot at a tie when Unitas spotted Eddie Hinton in the clear in the end zone on our last play of the game. His pass hit the cross bar and things ended with that. The score was 10-3 if you're interested. We held them to ten lousy points and still we couldn't win because our offense got us only three points.

After six games we had scored two shutouts and given up only thirty-four points, fewer than six a game, and were still only 4–2. I couldn't believe it. The best defensive team in the NFL, and we were in second place. We outscored the opposition, 135–34 and won only four out of six. That seems downright criminal.

I felt a lot better about my own performance against the Vikings. I got in some tremendous shots and I wasn't thinking so much about this damn thumb. I'm not sure how many tackles I made, but it must have been seven or eight. I also got a few good shots at some linemen coming through and was able to knock them out of the way so someone else could make the tackle and stop the play.

The cast wasn't interfering with my sleep anymore, and that was a relief. I have enough trouble sleeping as it is. If I get two good nights of sleep in a week, I'm happy. I start thinking about things and get excited about what's coming up the next day. Then a problem comes along and keeps me awake.

You might call me a worrier, although I think I'm more of a thinker than a worrier. I'm very intense about anything I'm involved in. I give everything all I've got. It keeps me awake, but I just can't help it. I'd like to be able to drop right off as soon as I lie down, but it often takes me an hour and a half or two hours to fall asleep at night. Last year I didn't sleep well at all, and before almost every game I felt tired.

We had one day less than usual to practice after the Viking game because it was played on a Monday night. They say that the teams that play the Monday night game often lose the following Sunday because it takes too much out of them and they don't have time to recover fully. I don't agree with that. It should never be true. Pro football players are big enough, old enough and ugly enough to know what they have to do to prepare for their next opponent. We knew after Minnesota. We knew we had to beat the Pittsburgh Steelers the next Sunday and we knew that to do this we had to stop their passer, Terry Bradshaw. We get paid to be prepared to beat them, whether we play the preceding Monday or not.

Pittsburgh likes to throw the screen pass and to run up the middle, so I was anticipating a busy afternoon. A middle linebacker must always be alert to both the screen and the draw play. They're both based on the unexpected—when you're prepared for a pass play. Swift reaction is essential, and your instant diagnosis had better be right or the play will gain plenty of yardage and the linebacker will be standing there exposed to the world.

The Colt linebackers are more active than linebackers on other teams, because we're expected to help the defensive backs on the pass patterns. We're required to drop back at least 10 yards, maybe 15. We try to back up that deep and in a hurry to cover the passing situation and watch for the sudden draw or screen.

Some teams form their draws late, taking three seconds

or so, which adds to the deception. They come running up through the middle and you come running back from your deep position to stop the play. There's a lineman blocking on you and you have to knock the lineman down or control him at full speed since the back is right behind him. He can cut either way on you. You have to get rid of the blocker and make the tackle or at least push the blocker back into the hole, jamming it shut and leaving the ballcarrier to be tackled by someone else. In the right situation and executed properly, the draw is damn tough to stop.

The reaction on a screen is similar. You drop back to help the backs on this pass play. Suddenly you realize it's a screen and you have to move fast. You have to get back to the line and either knife through the screen of blockers and make the tackle, or wipe out the screen so someone else can make the tackle.

They're both challenges to a middle linebacker, and Pittsburgh has the personnel to give a guy a full afternoon. Bradshaw is one of the top young quarterbacks to come into the league in my eight years as a pro. He's a good passer and he's a smart quarterback. He can make the screen work, and his best running back, Frenchy Fuqua, can make the draw work. Just my luck.

Pittsburgh's fortunes seem to run in the opposite direction from the Giants. While the Giants are on the decline, in Pittsburgh everything is looking up. Obviously they're getting good scouting, and Art Rooney always was willing to spend the money. His executives are making the right moves. The Steelers have been one of the doormats of the NFL about as long as anyone can remember, but they're on the rise now and in the next year or two they are going to put a lot of entries into that W column in the league standings. Funny how those things happen. For years the Giants were a powerhouse and the Steelers were the poor folks from the other side of the tracks. Now they've switched roles.

I thought earlier in the 1971 season, after a couple of games, that we would make it to the Super Bowl and play Minnesota, but the Vikings didn't turn out to be as good as I thought. They have the same problem we have—no offense.

As for ourselves, I said we would have either a great team or a good team. Well, we have a good team, not a great one. At least not yet. We have a great defense, and more and more people are coming to realize it and talk about it and write about it, but we won't have a great team until we can score consistently.

I hear more and more rumors that the Colts aren't long for Baltimore. Carroll Rosenbloom apparently has just about had it with the city in his requests that Memorial Stadium be improved. The state legislature came up with seven million dollars for the job, and that was more than a year ago.

The exhibition games in 1971 didn't help things any. Almost every other team in pro football plays before sell-out crowds, or almost, for its exhibition games. We played three exhibitions in Baltimore and averaged less than 15,000 people for each one. That's what the team that won the

Super Bowl draws for its home exhibitions. Meanwhile, thirty miles down at the other end of the Baltimore-Washington Parkway, the Washington Redskins, without a championship of any kind for over a quarter of a century, have been playing their exhibitions before 50,000 screaming loyal fans.

Nobody can understand it, not just people with the Colts but people with other teams, and the writers, too. For some reason Baltimore fans just won't support the team in exhibitions, and the owners claim this is where they must make their profit. They say expenses run so high that they can only break even on regular season games, and that exhibitions give them their profit.

Hell, the Orioles didn't even sell out the park for the last two games of the World Series. I just can't believe that, but it's true. I'm beginning to think we're winning too many championships in Baltimore for our own good. The Orioles have won the pennant four times in the last six years and the World Series twice. The Colts have the best won-lost record of any team in pro football for the past twelve years. And yet the Colts and the Orioles continue to suffer attendance problems. Maybe our teams are too good.

Winning championships by itself doesn't help any owner. He needs people coming into the ball park, and the Colts and the Orioles aren't getting them the way they should. You can't pay the bills with a championship ring or a pennant flying over your stadium.

So now things are almost at an impasse, and according to the rumor mill, we'll be moving after our lease on Memorial Stadium expires following the 1972 season. One rumor is that we may move to Columbia, a few miles out of Baltimore.

Another possibility is Tampa, Florida. I could take that. There are worse places than the west coast of Florida on the Gulf of Mexico. And that area has long been a real hotbed for pro football. Somebody will move in there sooner or later. They've got a stadium sitting there waiting for a team, and a metropolitan population of three million people doing the same. That kind of combination has been known to lure an owner before.

I wouldn't care much one way or the other. I want to open up a restaurant, and I have a team of consultants working on the financing involved and the matter of location. That would be the only factor in my reaction to a move. If I open a place in Baltimore and then we move, it could hurt, although maybe if I get a good enough start a move won't make much difference. And if we were to move to Tampa and I opened one down there in the right location, I could hit it big. The important thing is location. Maybe the whole issue will be resolved before I make any final decision on the restaurant question anyhow.

The question of artificial turf keeps coming up. The Players' Association wants to do away with the stuff completely, and maybe that's not a bad idea. I don't like that damn artificial turf any more. When we first started playing on it I thought it was pretty neat playing on a rug and having clean fingernails at the end of the game. But I don't feel that way any more. Artificial turf is too dangerous and causes too many injuries. I don't care what the people who make it say.

Grass is a more natural base on which to play football. The human being is an animal accustomed to living on the earth. His whole being has developed this way. He knows how to react on the ground and his balance is keyed to the ground.

Artificial turf is unnatural, so your body reacts to it unnaturally. That's why there are so many injuries. Sometimes when you make a cut you can feel it in your ankle or your knee. Other times you won't get a grip at all and you'll slide and pull a groin muscle. A lot of pro football players don't like it.

One of the original advantages, supposedly, to artificial turf was you would be able to play on it in the rain, but it hasn't worked out that way. It's like ice skating in the rain. You just slide across the turf the way you do on water skis. It makes any game a real farce.

I'll play on that stuff if I have to, but I don't like it. It hampers me in tackling someone bigger than I am or taking on one of the offensive linemen. On grass I'm able to slide my feet a little bit and I have a better angle to hold the guy up. But artificial turf keeps you from sliding on a dry field, and you get knocked over. It's not worth it—not just clean fingernails.

The burns you get from the stuff are something terrible. It tears right through the top layers of your skin to the second level, almost like a third-degree burn. I've seen three levels of skin come off when a guy skids on the stuff. I wear elbow pads for protection. The next time you see a game played on artificial turf on TV, notice how many of the players have elbow pads on to protect their arms. I saw John Mackey slide on artificial turf once after a fall, and when he came up his forearm was white. Then it started turning red, and that was blood. It was the rawest, bloodiest thing you ever saw.

Chapter 7

We weren't down yet. We beat the Steelers, 34–21, with Earl Morrall passing for 286 yards and three touchdowns. And he played only slightly more than half the game. Earl hit Willie Richardson twice for TDs in the first half. Then he opened the third quarter with a 60-yard scoring pass to Ray Perkins. And he set up our first touchdown of the game with a 64-yard pass to Perkins. What quarterback problem?

Don McCafferty gave Earl the rest of the day off early in the third quarter, but John Unitas couldn't get us any more points. And one of his passes was intercepted with one minute and fifty seconds left to play to set up their final touchdown. The Steelers scored only one touchdown on their own against our defense. It was a three-yard pass from Terry Bradshaw to Ron Shank midway through the third quarter, when we were ahead, 34–7. It was the first touchdown pass scored against us all year.

We stopped the Steelers cold on the ground with 31 yards total rushing. And even with that they got only 155 yards passing, and most of that was short stuff that we were conceding because of our big lead. In 1970 Pittsburgh was fourth in the American Conference in total offense and first in passing with Bradshaw, so we were stopping a pretty respectable offense. The Steelers are a coming team, no question about that. You can't kiss them off anymore. They're going to keep getting better. Their fans may be in for some happy times.

I wasn't totally satisfied with my own performance. That damn cast still bugged me, though. Once I had a shot at their running back, Frenchy Fuqua. He had a lineman coming through the hole ahead of him. I submarined the blocker and grabbed Fuqua's leg, but I could hold on only with my left arm because of the cast on the right. He got away for about five yards. Another time Bradshaw rolled out and I had him dead, but I couldn't hold him, again because of the cast.

Those two plays typify what was happening to me. I was making the moves, reacting well, hitting well, getting the ballcarrier, getting to the receiver on a pass play into my territory on our zone defense, doing everything I should. But the damn cast was undermining me too many times. It's frustrating as hell to know you did everything right on a play and were the guy making the first hit on a ballcarrier, only to have him slip away because you're playing with one hand.

These misses gnawed at me. I played the whole Pittsburgh game and made some good tackles and some other good plays, but those two misses—out of the whole sixty minutes—ruined my entire weekend.

Two days to relax at my farm. I get down there every chance I have. I'm a loner. I prefer to be by myself or with my family. I'm uncomfortable in crowds, which may sound crazy coming from a guy who makes his living in a goldfish bowl with 60,000 people judging his performance every week, and maybe millions more on television. But even in a game I feel I have my territory and I'm alone in that territory. That's one of the things that helps me make the play when the ballcarrier or pass receiver comes my way. He's coming into my territory and he has no right there and I'm going to get him and make him pay for trespassing on my turf. Even when I was a kid in Rockville, I was a loner and preferred it that way, just as I do now. We had a large woods behind our house, and I'd go out there with my dog and we would be in our own private world for hours on end. I could have lived forever in that woods, and I still feel that way. My dislike for crowds is balanced by my love for nature. So if I'm alone in a woods or on my farm or in some other unspoiled natural setting, I am a contented man.

My farm covers forty-four acres near Leesburg, Virginia, about ninety minutes from where my wife Marty and I were renting a town house in Columbia, and only about forty-five minutes from my old home town of Rockville. I bought the place with my earnings from our first

Super Bowl, and now my parents live on it year-round.

From the back windows you can gaze peacefully at the Blue Ridge Mountains of Virginia. The view of the Blue Ridge is more beautiful than ever in autumn, with the mountains exploding with color as the leaves change in the early November days.

We have a natural spring on the property and we get all of our water from it. The house, which Dad and I have worked on for almost four years now, is frame and covered with yellow aluminum siding with black shutters. It was built before the Civil War, and that's another reason I like it. I have great respect for things like that. Dad and I remodeled a lot of the interior, with a contractor doing what we couldn't. We have three bedrooms on the second floor, a fourth in the attic, a big kitchen, a dining room and a living room, a basement recreation room with a fireplace, plus a laundry room and a combination shop-pantry.

We have a front porch where you can sit and look at the meadows and woods that stretch out before you, and a white fence that runs along the road, 700 feet away. We have a corn field and apple orchards and pear orchards, three barns and a garage and a silo, plus thirty-five head of cattle and a hay field.

The farm is one of my great rewards from pro football. I look out over my forty-four acres, with horses and cows grazing among the autumn-colored trees, and I don't feel "dehumanized" in the least. On the contrary, football has been my vehicle to the most uplifting qualities of human experience.

Some day Marty and I will live there, and we get there every week during the season to visit Mom and Dad and enjoy the tranquility and the privacy. At the farm, there are no missed tackles.

Dad commutes every day to his job with the D.C. Transit Company in Washington, where he is a traffic supervisor. It takes him an hour and a half each way, but he feels it's worth it. He and Mom were ready to leave the city anyhow. They were thinking about a farm, and so was I, and when that Super Bowl money came my way, I went shopping for a farm.

I found it advertised in the paper. When I bought it, the house had no aluminum siding, no central heat, only one working bathroom, no storm windows, no closets, and the floors were in awful condition, the barns needed ceiling beams, and I spent $2,000 in fencing.

The farm is a good investment too, both long-range and short-range. After going there following the win over Pittsburgh, Dad and I made $2,000 net profit by selling those thirty-five head of cattle. And it's a good tax write-off for me, which any professional athlete needs. We make good money, but we don't make it for long. And the age at which we stop making it is the age at which most other professionals are just beginning to get into the respectable salary brackets. It's something that the nation's tax laws should allow for, but they don't, except that you can take your salary on a deferred basis over a period of years so you're not paying a whole chunk of taxes each year on your full salary.

The other method that I use is to purchase real estate. In addition to the farm, I own fourteen acres of land near Olney, in Montgomery County, the same county where my home town of Rockville is located. I own a house in Rockville, which I bought with my best friend and old school buddy, Kenny Tuchtan. And Kenny and I own a lot in the Bahamas. I also have a home on Route 28 near Rockville and some light industrial property in Rockville and part of the Goodyear Building, also in Rockville.

I cut my tax bill in half last year by buying land. In contrast, I plowed all of my 1971 Super Bowl money into the stock market, about $18,000 worth. And I've since told my broker to unload it for me, thirteen days before President Nixon's Phase Two went into effect. That stock market makes me nervous. I don't like to gamble. Maybe that's why I'm not much of a cardplayer. Taking wild chances with money makes me nervous. Give me those good, safe land investments every time.

But I can't really kid myself all the time while I'm at the farm. I'm never really able to shake the football out of me, and I guess that's the way it should be. Even with all the fun you have in this business—and it is a business—and even with all the recognition you get and the money you make, sometimes you find yourself wishing you were a truck driver or a sales clerk and when five o'clock comes you go home and never have a reason to think about your job until nine o'clock the next morning.

Then I found myself thinking about that Pittsburgh game again. Earl Morrall showed us he still has what it takes. But I wasn't confident he would be consistent. To win championships you must be consistent. There are no inconsistent champions.

I took a sleeping pill the night before the game, plus a tranquilizer to wear off the sleeping pill's effects so I wouldn't have a hangover. I slept well and was plenty rested for the game, and on the basis of this experience

Dave Meggyesy can now say I'm a dope addict. I needed that rest. It's the first time this season I've gotten a good rest the night before a game.

I suppose I'd sleep a lot better in a shed or some place where I wouldn't have to worry about untidying my room; where I could just flop around in a shack in the woods and rough it and not worry about the appearance of my surroundings. I've always been a sloppy guy around the house anyhow. It used to bother the hell out of Kenny Tuchtan when we had our house in Rockville after we had both graduated from college and I was starting out with the Colts and Kenny was getting started in the real estate business. He used to make me close the door to my room.

I remember I used to have a blue shag rug on the floor in my room. I'd walk around the house in my white socks and track that blue stuff all over the hall and into the bathroom and the living room and everywhere. Kenny used to follow me around, picking up the blue rug shavings off the floor behind me. We were the original odd couple.

Bubba Smith and his date came over to dinner recently. He ate everything—the meal, the table, the chairs, the plates, everything. I hardly had a bite or two of anything because of Bubba. He says his mother used to refer to Bubba and his brother as "my two walruses." When you see him—six feet, eight inches and 270 pounds—you can understand why even a mother would say a thing like that.

Jimmy Bailey, one of our tackles, and his wife came by after dinner. He weighs 260. And damned if he and Bubba didn't have to sit on the sofa—both of them at once. They couldn't sit on separate pieces of furniture. Five hundred and thirty pounds on our new sofa. Marty and I had been married only eight months, and I'm confident our marriage will survive, but I wasn't so sure about our sofa.

Chuck Hughes of the Detroit Lions collapsed and died right on the field during a game, and the whole League was rocked. In Baltimore the next Sunday they had a memorial service for him before our game with Pittsburgh. The players weren't really as upset about it as their wives were. We don't think about that sort of thing very much, and when something like this happens we figure it's a rarity, tragic but a rarity. Certainly you can't be a pro football player and go out on that field every Sunday worried that you might die during the game. Football doesn't work that way, and neither does life.

We finally had to end those two lovely days off at the farm and head back into the hard turf at Memorial Stadium and go to work to get ready for the Los Angeles Rams and Roman Gabriel. We were still in that undesirable position where we had to win every week and hope that somebody would come along and knock off Miami, or else we'd have to do it ourselves.

It would be the first time I'd be playing against Gabriel since we beat them in 1968 to take the Western Conference lead. The Associated Press voted me Defensive Player of the Week after that game. Their story about it called me "tough, quick, volatile" and said I won the award for my "savage treatment" of Gabriel. They didn't even call me an animal or a mad dog. But that was more than three years ago. They've called me those things enough times since to make up for it.

Even the Los Angeles papers seemed up for this one. The *Herald-Examiner* had a piece by Steve Bisheff saying, "The outdoor zoo known as Memorial Stadium doesn't worry the Rams as much as the middle linebacker they call 'The Animal.'" There's the animal image again. He quoted Billy Ray Smith, who retired a couple of years ago after playing tackle for us for ten years, as saying "Mike eats the panes right out of the bus windows on the way to practice. He chews the face bars right off his helmet."

And our coach, Don McCafferty, was quoted as saying, "If we had twenty-two Mike Curtises, we could send them to the stadium and tell them to bring back a winner while we sat and watched the game on TV." I was glad to read that McCafferty said that. I would have to remind the front office of that when my contract came up for renewal.

Chapter 8

Among the 57,722 fans out to watch us take on the Rams were Vice-President Agnew and Ethel Kennedy. I suppose Dave Meggyesy would tell you they were engaging in a "sexual frenzy," too. Out on the field we were engaging in our own kind of frenzy, and sex had nothing to do with it. We played football and we beat the Rams, 24–17. It would have been 24–10 if it hadn't been for an incompetent call by one of the officials.

The Vice-President visited our dressing room before the game, and the crowd there was almost as big as the one in the stands. He was surrounded by five Secret Service agents looking suspiciously and suspicious. I didn't know whether they were protecting him or whether some other guys were supposed to be protecting Agnew from them. I talked to the Vice-President briefly at my locker, the second time I have met him. I first met him when he was Governor of Maryland. He used to come to every Colts game. He's still a big football fan and a close follower of our performances.

Howard Cosell was there too, only slightly less prominent than the Vice-President of the United States. Cosell was ribbing everyone, the way he does each week before the Monday night TV game. Agnew asked about my TV commercials and about my thumb. It seemed the thumb was doing better than the commercials, which seemed to have faded from view. I wanted to ask the Vice-President if he uses the hair tonic mentioned in my commercials, but I decided I'd better show some sense of propriety, even at the risk of damaging my animalistic image.

Cosell is always in the dressing room before Monday night games telling each player, "I'm going to expose you for the type of player you are." The players just shout back, "Rap on, Cosell, rap on." Meredith is always in there too, the happy clown, saying, "Say hi to me, Curtis. Don't forget to speak to me. Then I'll give you a plug on TV."

Meredith, Cosell and Frank Gifford are all pretty much the same as the general impression fans have of them. Meredith is the happy analyst, the former Dallas quarterback who knows what he's watching and can enrich the viewer's enjoyment of the game by passing new information along without taking himself too seriously. Gifford is the calm, thoroughly professional commentator, the former star running back for the Giants whose knowledge runs deep, who keeps a check on his emotions and also brings great poise and decorum to his job. Cosell is, well —Cosell is Cosell. You know it. I know it. He knows it. He's a smart cookie who can ride hell out of people, but he can take it and he does. The players give him a pretty good riding every Monday night in the dressing room before he goes on the air. Maybe that explains some of the things he says.

I don't get to watch the TV reporters much because we're always playing. Two of the men I respect most among newspaper reporters are Shirley Povich of the *Washington Post* and Tony Atchison of the *Washington Star*. Cameron Snyder of the *Baltimore Sun* is another. They are thoroughly professional and approach their assignments without bias. They can use the Queen's English, and they're not lazy. They're willing to spend whatever time is needed to get the story and they're willing to listen while they're getting it. The result is honest, fair, competent and intelligent reporting by honest, fair, competent and intelligent men. As George Gobel, the comedian, always says, "You can't hardly find them no more."

Reporters decide my fate. What they say forms impressions, and impressions form reputations and players get paid on the basis of their reputations. I have a lot of respect for the good ones, and no respect for the others —the majority. Most reporters for both TV and the papers seem satisfied with superficial stories which too often seem to be written off other stories. In other words, they're just rewriting someone else or they're writing the first thing that comes to their minds or they're writing something to support their preconceived notions without letting the facts get in their way.

I know Agnew blew the lid off things a few years ago when he said what he did about the news media, but a lot of us in public life have to agree with some of his complaints—entertainers, political figures, professional athletes, astronauts and anyone else whose activities and job performances are evaluated by newsmen for all the world. That's a serious responsibility reporters have, and they can ruin a guy's career and his spirit and break a guy. Or they can create a cardboard superman, a ballplayer who really isn't as good as the impressionable press might think he is at first glance. How many rave notices have you read about a guy hitting .400 in April? He's here to stay, he's a veteran who is finally arriving, or he's an "unheralded rookie" who is "threatening to become the league's newest superstar." And by August he's back on the bench, or playing for Topeka.

The same kind of thing happens in football. You read in the early days of training camp about the free agent who gives promise of moving the established veteran out of the starting lineup. Two weeks later he's cut. How many times have you asked, "Hey, whatever happened to that kid who was looking so good in training camp?" Then you were told, "He was cut." Or, "He's on the taxi squad."

You'll read that your team lost because the running back fumbled the handoff. Isn't it also possible the quarterback made a sloppy handoff? Or you'll read that the quarterback's pass was intercepted, but you won't read that the receiver ran his pattern all wrong. Or you'll read that the opponents' receiver caught the touchdown pass that won the game right in front of the cornerback, but what you won't read is that the cornerback was helping someone else out on the play, because he saw his defensive team-mate miss his assignment; and the cornerback was making a great try at stopping the play when it wasn't even his man who caught the ball.

The fantastic influence of the press on individual careers and individual lives was never shown more dramatically than in what happened to Roger Maris after he hit those sixty-one home runs in 1961. The pressures on him were enough to snap a lesser man, and they were the pressures generated largely by the news media. Maris didn't snap, but he became a changed man, especially in his dealings with reporters and in some of his views. Likewise Duane Thomas. And Vida Blue.

Our careers as professional athletes are dependent to a large degree on what the reporters say about us. It doesn't seem right. I'm not sure reporters realize the power of their typewriters and their microphones—power to create people and power to destroy people.

Everyone was up for the Rams game. Our performance showed it. We played a good game against a good, strong team, and it was a good sign of what lay ahead. If we could beat the Rams convincingly, and we did, we had a good chance against anyone. The Rams showed us the best running attack we'd seen all year, but they still gained only 108 yards on the ground and that's not an unusually high total. Gabriel did not appear sharp to me, even though he had 154 yards passing.

I made my biggest play of the year when I punched the ball from Larry Smith's arm, and Ted Hendricks scooped it up and ran 31 yards for an important touchdown, looking like a "Mad Stork" every step of the way. It broke a 10–10 tie in the third quarter and moved us ahead to stay.

Controversy seems to find me, and this play produced some more. A story in a Los Angeles paper after the game quoted their freshman coach, Tommy Prothro, as saying the play wouldn't have happened if it hadn't been for my cast. That's true. But then he said more. The article, by Mal Florence of the *Los Angeles Times*, described the league rules on casts, a subject I'm familiar with because the officials tell me every week not to use the cast as a weapon. Our trainers have to follow the rules closely in bandaging my hand and arm before the game. Then the officials inspect it themselves. So the subject was not new to me.

But Prothro said I used the cast "like a club" and was "fortunate" to force the fumble and that I barely made physical contact. Art McNally, the supervisor of NFL officials, was quoted as saying, "A cast must be completely covered with three-eighths of an inch of foam rubber so it isn't dangerous. I wasn't in Baltimore Monday, but I was there the week before for the Pittsburgh game and Curtis' cast met the specifications."

Damn right it did. And if it will make Prothro feel any better, I sure as hell would have preferred playing without the cast. I didn't have a cast on three years ago when we beat the Rams and I was named Defensive Player of the Week. I wasn't able to have that kind of a game this time because of the cast. Otherwise, I might have played a helluva lot better against the Rams. So Prothro should be glad I wore the cast, even if it did cost him a touchdown. As for his charge that I barely made contact on the play, he should look at the pictures. There was a sequence of three pictures of the play in the *Baltimore Sun*, and the first picture clearly shows me with my right arm wrapped all the way across Smith's chest to his left arm, the arm carrying the ball. If wrapping your arm around a guy's whole front isn't making contact, what is?

Prothro is all wet when he says I used the cast like a club. I told Tony Atchison of the *Washington Star* in the dressing room after the game how it really happened: "I was going to grab Smith, but the ball shot out of his arm. I knew the thumb cast had hit it, even though I didn't feel it at the time. That ball really went up in the air. It was my biggest play of the year, even bigger than my two interceptions against Buffalo, because it helped us to win the first in a streak of four tough games—the Rams, Jets, Dolphins and Raiders."

When the ball popped out of Smith's arms, I didn't even know it. The first I knew about it was when I saw the ball high in the air, and I guessed what had happened. But I didn't know it at the moment, because I was surprised. Prothro doesn't have to believe that, but it's the truth. I'll remember Prothro's crying the next time we play the Rams—and I'll be playing with two hands.

I thought the Rams might pick on me. They tried three times. Once the guard hit me and I hit their runner, Willie Ellison, who almost tore my shoulder off, but I was able to make the play. Then Larry Smith went inside guard and I got him. The third time I closed the hole by hitting the guard with my right shoulder. The runner had to go outside and someone else got him because they were double-teaming me.

Frank Gifford said some nice things about my coverage on a Gabriel pass into the end zone. The deep back had the receiver covered in the end zone, and I was in front of the receiver under the goal post. My friends tell me Gifford credited my presence in front of the receiver with persuading Gabriel not to throw and risk an interception, so he threw it away, out of the end zone. I was only where I was supposed to be in our standard zone coverage on a pass play, but it's nice to know a respected guy like Gifford is saying nice things about you to a coast-to-coast TV audience. The publicity helps. I hope the coaches, the guys who select the players for the All-Pro team, were watching—and listening.

Norman Bulaich just wasn't up to par. He did more blocking than usual and they laid off calling his number any more than necessary. The reason was that he had been up until four o'clock in the morning with the flu, throwing up and all the rest. He threw up three times during the game behind our bench, and again in the dressing room at the half. I hope he made sure he was out of camera range so the national TV audience didn't see him losing his stomach. Even so, almost 60,000 fans in the stadium had a chance to see it.

I was disappointed with the season so far. I'd have to straighten up fast, cast or no cast, or I wouldn't make the wire service All-Pro team or the Pro Bowl or anything else. I couldn't continue to remind myself that I was playing with a cast on a broken bone. Forget the cast. I had to play well by my own professional standards, thumb or no thumb.

I had one of the pins removed after the Rams game, and the cast would come off in another week or so. Then I would play with a much smaller and lighter plexiglass cast. Before they took that pin out, they gave me a needle to deaden the pain, but the pain-killer almost deadened me instead of the pain. I've had needles in my shoulders, my knees and my ankles, but they were nothing like what I had for the pin. After the pain-killer, the doctor cut the skin with a scalpel and pulled out the pin gently from its location between the first and second joint. It took only five or ten minutes. The other pin was in the part of the bone on the heel of the hand. It would have to stay there until after the season.

That last TD by the Rams shouldn't have been a touchdown at all. We should have won the game 24–10. Matt Maslowski grabbed a pass in the corner of the end zone in the last minute. But he had one foot out of bounds. His left foot came down entirely on the white out-of-bounds stripe. If Tom Matte hadn't just scored to give us a two-touchdown lead, that play would have made the game a tie—on a call that was just plain wrong. My friends say the play was rerun about a half-dozen times on TV and that Howard Cosell, Don Meredith and Frank Gifford were unanimous in saying Maslowski was out of bounds.

I don't know when Rozelle is going to do something about the incompetent officials in pro football, but he'd better do something fast. One of these times there's going to be a classic boner by a referee in a playoff game or the Super Bowl and it will decide the game and the bad call will bring national embarrassment to the game. Maybe then Rozelle will start to do something.

One of the things he ought to think about is using instant replay to help with the decisions. Some people say this takes the fun out of the game, or the human element. Baloney. It makes the decisions by the officials fair and accurate, and how can you knock that? You could have a replay camera on the sidelines, with an official whose job it would be to monitor the showing of the tape and to make a ruling based on what he saw. Or he could be responsible for determining when the officials on the field must go to the sidelines to consult the replay for their decision. What the hell, even in baseball the home-plate umpire can make a call but then confer with the third- or first-base umpire if he thinks they had a better view. We've got the technology and the equipment to use instant replay on the sidelines, with the officials controlling it to make sure the play is called the right way, but what does the League do? Nothing.

Another thing Rozelle ought to do to correct this lousy officiating is not exactly revolutionary, but it works: fire the incompetents. A firing here and there does wonders for the efficiency of the surviving employees in any organization. If a guy can get this worked up about poor officiating after a game his team won, then you know something's wrong. And there is something wrong. If Pete Rozelle doesn't do something, he's going to be awfully embarrassed one of these days—in front of a whole nation.

We got ready to play the Jets again at Shea Stadium in New York. You remember the Jets, don't you? They're the team that hasn't beaten us since we met in the Super Bowl. Of course, we figured to beat them once more. But that's the kind of situation you have to watch—when you're coming off an impressive victory over a strong team and you're going up against a decidedly weaker team and you're the heavy favorite. That kind of situation always make coaches nervous—and me, too. Even so, we really did figure to beat hell out of them. They didn't have a quarterback because Namath was still out with that knee, and now they didn't have a running game, either. They had a lot of injuries. But every time I feel safe about playing the Jets, I remember that damned Super Bowl.

Maybe McCafferty should always do what he did before we played the Jets in our first game with them after losing the Super Bowl. He called a Saturday meeting and showed us that whole agonizing game on film. Then, without a word, he adjourned the meeting. We beat hell out of them.

I didn't have much of a chance for All-Pro the way things were going in 1971. I just hoped I would make the Pro Bowl. So I just concentrated with the rest of the guys on making the Super Bowl, and the individual honors would have to wait until next year. I just didn't have a very good first half. People were nice enough to say I was doing great with a cast on my arm, but to me I'm not doing great if I don't play as well as I would without the cast.

I would just have to wait until next season for the All-Pro and maybe for the Pro Bowl, too, even though I've been voted both twice already. Maybe the guys who make the picks would allow for my thumb, even if I didn't allow for it myself. Willie Lanier of Kansas City seemed to be my chief competition. And Dick Butkus of the Bears wasn't playing that well, from what I heard, because of his bum leg. But even if I missed the honors in 1971, I'd have to make sure I played well enough in 1972 to make all the honors I could. For one good reason: that was when my four-year contract ended. When I signed my current contract I was an outside linebacker. Now I'm the middle linebacker, with more responsibility and more of a leadership role. That figures. In the thick of the action, the whole defense tends to react the way the middle linebacker does. So I would have to have one helluva year in 1972 to make sure I got paid not only as a middle linebacker, but as an outstanding one.

Every little bit of recognition, every mention of your name on TV, helps you at contract time. It helps determine the amount of the fee you draw for personal appearances and endorsements. Recognition is the key to everything, assuming, of course, that you perform well as a player.

But the best recognition for any of us would have been to go to New Orleans in January and really win big in the Super Bowl. Then I'd feel fulfilled, convinced that we are the best and that we demonstrated it to the whole country with an impressive victory in the championship game.

But this was only November. And there was a possibility—I had to face it—that the team that beat us in our first Super Bowl could keep us from going there again if they whipped us on the Sunday coming.

The anxieties in this business could get to a guy if he let them.

Chapter 9

If it's not whether you win or lose but how you play the game that counts, then we have real problems.

We beat the Jets again—whipped hell out of 'em. The score? Oh, it was 14–13. You might say the game was a lot closer than the score indicates. The Jets led at the half, 7–0, and they would have won the game if it hadn't been for a blocked field goal by Jerry Logan and an extra point that was blocked by Ted Hendricks. God, what a frustrating year.

I thought the refs were their usual incompetent selves, but that's not news either. I'll say one thing about those guys—they're impartial. They're lousy on both sides. After the game Weeb Ewbank ran onto the field looking for the officials. He wanted to give them the game ball.

The tendency in that kind of a game, with the other team's number one quarterback injured, is to say that with him in the lineup they would have won the game. But I'm not sure that's entirely true. If Joe Namath had been playing, maybe our guys would have bore down a lot harder. As it was, the team was dead, flatter than I thought possible. But if we had been going against Joe Willie, we might have been more up for the game, including the offense. That was the main reason for our lousy performance—nobody was up. The coaches thought we were looking past the Jets to Miami, our next opponent, and they were right. We were supposed to be able to beat the Jets by fourteen points. As it turned out, we barely escaped with our season's hopes still intact. And if it hadn't been for those two key blocked kicks. . . .

Namath is one of the guys I respect most as an athlete. He's the greatest passer in the game today. If he were the Colts' quarterback, we'd never lose a game. Unitas is a better team leader, though. When Namath throws a pass, he falls to the ground and curls up into a fetal position, because he's afraid of hurting those knees again. After Unitas throws, he stands right there and shows the opposition he's not afraid of them. He gets decked a lot, but his teammates see his guts as he's standing there like Custer at Little Big Horn defying the other team, and they remember this about him and respond to it, and this makes John a great leader.

Namath's injury wouldn't make any difference in how hard I hit him, although it might make a difference in where I hit him. If he's playing, it means he's ready to take the punishment, and no team can be expected to take it easy on him. That's flirting with defeat. But I would try to avoid his knees. I would try to tackle him around the shoulders. But if he tried to run, I would have to dive for him. And then maybe my only option would be to go for his legs, knees or no knees.

Some guys, unfortunately, would deliberately go for his knees. You find creatures like that in any sport, those who try to hurt you intentionally. I don't agree with that. (I realize that such consideration jeopardizes my "animal" and "mad dog" image.) I don't think it's fair game to hit a guy in the knees to get him out of the game. If you want to get him out of the game, hit him in the head when you're coming straight for him. That's a fair shot. (Now my animal image is repaired.) Tackle him high or clothesline him. But don't go for his knees. That's a cheap shot. That's not even professional. It's like being a mercenary.

Getting back to ole Joe Willie, though—he'll always come back. I don't think one injury will ever rack him up for good. Maybe the accumulation of injuries will end it for him if he can't throw the ball well any more, or things become too much of a physical effort for him, but one particular injury will never end his career.

When he got it last season, in one of the Jets' early exhibition games, we were playing at home the same night. Because of his importance to the sport, and the familiarity of his name in Baltimore, they announced the news of his injury on the public address system at the stadium. Guess how some Baltimore fans reacted. They cheered. Let us assume they were the vocal minority.

Except for a broken wrist in 1970, Namath's injuries

have been confined to his knees as far as I know. Unitas can top that with no trouble. He's been injured all over. People talk with respect about how brave Namath is, and that's true, but he's no braver than John Unitas. No one is. Unitas had a serious knee injury in 1965, the year Tom Matte filled in at quarterback with the plays taped to his wrist. John has broken about every rib in his body, and he has suffered jammed fingers and a broken nose and a broken elbow. Once he broke a rib and punctured his lung and he had to have a tube inserted to drain the fluid from his lung. He played two weeks later.

Football is like any other sport or any other business. There are right ways and wrong ways to go about it. Some people will play it straight and others won't. If you're a pro football player and you play defense, you soon learn who and what to look out for. Blockers cheat in a variety of ways. One way they do it is to tackle you. The blocker knocks you down, then wraps his arms around you and holds you, just as if you were the ballcarrier. Only you're on the ground and he's keeping you out of the play. Winston Hill, a tackle for the Jets, is notorious for this.

Some blockers will go for your knees from the blind side. Or if you get in front of them they'll clip you, taking a chance they won't get caught. Or if you get past them and they've fallen to the ground, they'll stretch their legs out and try to leg-whip you. Officials could call a holding penalty on offensive linemen every play of the game if they wanted to.

Defensive players have their own variety of cheating ways. They can twist the ballcarrier's knee or they can jump on the pile after the play is finished or they can come running into the action with a cocked fist or an elbow

110

that just happens to be sticking out there and catches someone's jaw.

But just because some people try these things doesn't mean all of us do. I'd say only about five per cent of the players in pro football could be called dirty players. That doesn't seem especially high to me. You probably find the same percentage of cheaters in any professional group. It's just that much more conspicuous in sports. When you get caught cheating, the official drops a bright yellow flag, and the TV camera zooms in on it as he signals the infraction to 60,000 people in the stadium and millions watching it on TV. It's harder to get caught padding a professional fee or cutting corners on someone's automobile repairs or jacking up prices in a store. But people in other occupations do those things, and maybe the percentage is higher than the five per cent I estimate for pro football.

I took a tranquilizer and a muscle relaxer the night before the Jets' game and got ten hours of sleep. I slept so well I was late for our nine o'clock meeting Sunday morning. I got there at 9:30. Bill Curry had called me at eight, as he usually did before leaving for church. I always said I was awake. Then I'd go back to sleep. This time it would cost me twenty-five or fifty bucks.

There was some improvement in my performance, as a result of a different thumb cast. Lately I was more concerned about the cast than my thumb. That's progress. The new cast was lighter and more flexible so I could grip things better—things like blockers and runners and pass receivers and quarterbacks.

Marty came up for the game, and Ewbank's organization stuck her in the boondocks way out near the rim of

Shea Stadium. Happily, she was rescued by Carroll Rosenbloom, the Colts' owner, and Don Klosterman, our general manager, who invited her to sit in their box. Marty rubbed elbows and chatted with Ed Sullivan, Gordon MacRae, the wife of Astronaut Scott Carpenter and some other wheels. After the game Carroll took us to dinner at Trader Vic's. I had been there the night before with Marty and a friend of ours. Playing the smoothie, I sprang for the check. Dinner for three, with one drink apiece. Sixty dollars, please. Sixty bucks! Man, that town is something else. So when we went with Rosenbloom to the same place the next night, I let him be the smoothie.

The day after we beat the Jets I gave an off-the-record talk to a luncheon sponsored by a group of advertisers for *Sport* magazine on the occasion of its twenty-fifth anniversary. I was asked what I thought about Dave Meggyesy's book. I said I thought it was a microcosm of the unrest in today's society. My feeling, and I told the people at the luncheon this, is that any player can do what he wants to as long as he doesn't hurt the team. That's my attitude, and the attitude of many others, but that's not Meggyesy's attitude. Not only that, he makes you think his own experiences are the experiences of every pro football player. It just isn't so, and that's what makes his book so misleading. He writes as if the St. Louis Cardinals are typical. Well, they're not. And Dave Meggyesy isn't typical either.

The people at the luncheon asked me who the best linebacker in pro football is. I told them Willie Lanier of the Kansas City Chiefs. They asked me when John Unitas would regain the quarterback job and I told them when he performs well enough to deserve it. I think even John would say the same thing.

We returned home Monday and took Marty's grandmother to visit relatives in Philadelphia. It's the only good reason I know for visiting Philadelphia. We stayed for several hours and I amused them by behaving like a human being. One guy even said, "Gee, you don't act like I thought you would."

I said, "How did you think I would act?"

He said, "Well, you know, you read a lot of things. . . ."

I said, "You want me to tear up the house? I can if you want, but it will cost you some money in repair bills."

Now the season would be starting, because our next stop was Miami, the team we had to beat to win our division.

Frankly, I thought we could beat Miami, despite the Griese-Warfield combination. Bubba Smith and John Mackey were looking forward to getting another shot at Don Shula, our old coach. They weren't too happy under Shula at Baltimore, and when he bailed out and headed for Miami they saw fit to say a few things in public. Now, whenever we play the Dolphins, they try to show Shula their ability, and that's a plus for us.

The trend toward low-scoring games seemed to be holding, if the 1971 season was any barometer. For example, the Vikings, who had a 7–2–0 record midway through the season, averaged only fourteen points a game. In their game against the Packers they had a total of 87 yards to Green Bay's 301 yards. Yet the Vikings won, 3–0, on a field goal.

There are reasons for this. In my opinion, the defenses are more sophisticated than they were in the past. Against the zone defense, with every man covering a designated territory, scoring isn't as easy as it used to be. This could be a good thing. A game with a lopsided score is never as exciting as a close contest. Defense *should* catch up with offense. It heightens the challenge of football and keeps everyone on his toes.

On a related subject, some people complain about too many tie games. They would like to see a provision for the two-point conversion and sudden death in the event of a tie. I disagree on both counts. The argument is that the two-pointer would add excitement to "the pros' dullest play—the extra point." All I can say is we won a game on "the pros' dullest play" when Ted Hendricks blocked that extra point try against the Jets. There was nothing dull about that.

Hank Stram of the Kansas City Chiefs would like to see either the two-pointer or sudden death. Fourteen sudden deaths in eight weeks? Maybe you could put the two-pointer into the Super Bowl, but the games leading up to that are a thinning-out process anyway, so sudden deaths are just not necessary until the decisive day—or maybe in the playoffs. Man, we play six exhibition games, fourteen regular season games and, if we go all the way, three post-season games. Last year we had to play in the College All-Star game, too. With sudden deaths possible in every one of those, a guy could get pretty tired.

"The pros' dullest play" also became one of the most talked-about plays of the year. Dick Butkus, the Bears' middle linebacker, caught a desperation pass from Bobby Douglass and beat the Redskins with it. It happened like this: The snap from center for the extra point try was messed up and Douglass had to scramble. He wound up back at the 35-yard line and let fly with the football. Butkus had lined up as an end on that play to block on the left side for his team's attempted kick. He grabbed the pass from Douglass in the end zone for the extra point and the Bears had their upset victory.

My old friend and high school coach, Roy Lester, was about to get fired as head football coach at Maryland University. I visited Roy at College Park. He was really bitter. He said he couldn't discipline his players because the University's administration wouldn't back him up. One player blasted him publicly in the school paper. Lester felt that students who don't want to work should be dropped from the team, but again the school wouldn't back him up. What kind of nonsense is this anyway? How can you run anything without some degree of discipline? I don't say you need a Vince Lombardi to run roughshod over these college kids, but hell, you have to have something resembling discipline.

I played for Roy Lester for three years, and I never felt deprived of my rights or dehumanized. Who runs even an office without discipline? I'll bet the President of the University of Maryland has discipline in his office. Or does he let the employees come and go when they want and work when they feel like it and not work at all if they don't want to? I hate to imagine what some of our college students are going to think when they get out into the real world and find out that man does not live by protest alone.

Poor Roy was taking stomach medicine and tranquilizers for severe headaches and sleeping at the stadium a couple of times a week because he was putting in so many hours. And the word from the campus was that if Roy Lester had the support from the college administration that winning basketball coach Lefty Driesell does, Lester would have a winner, too. Instead, they didn't support him. They sided with the players—even the ones who went over his head without talking to him first. Then they talked about firing him because he couldn't produce a winner. Man, oh man!

Speaking of college football, Notre Dame's players recently voted not to go to a bowl game. Good for them. Some say they felt they wouldn't get a bid from a major bowl. Some say they weren't sure they would win in a bowl game. I don't care what the reason was. What I think is important is they voted not to go.

I think the college season is long enough as it is. We never went to a bowl when I was at Duke, and I was glad of it. Players who have been in bowl games tell me it's an awful load on them scholastically. They leave their studies behind them, they practice starting early in December and have to neglect their school work while classes are still going on. Then when they leave for the site of the game, most of them do not take their books with them. They could be made to study two or three or even four hours a day and keep up with their classwork while they're preparing for the bowl game, but the coaches never worry about such things. That's why I'm against bowl games.

To me, education comes first in college. Football is only a part of going to college, and not the most important part. It should be considered an extension of the intramural sports program. I'm really a purist on this.

Somehow I can't get that excited about college football anymore. I follow Duke and Maryland and not much else. I couldn't tell you from one week to the next which teams are in the top ten. College football is not as lively to watch as pro football is. The action isn't as fast, the execution isn't as great and the scoring isn't as explosive. It's just not the same game, and it is just too tame by comparison. As if all that weren't enough, college football fans seldom get to see their own game on TV.

Chapter 10

The Baltimore Colts and the President of the United States shared a similar experience at this point in the season: We both got thrown for a loss in Miami.

The Colts lost to the Dolphins, 17–14, and President Nixon lost to the AFL-CIO, 1–0, with George Meany the one.

For the Colts, the afternoon couldn't have been more frustrating. We marched up and down the field early in the game, scoring a touchdown on a long drive after the opening kickoff. With Unitas guiding the offense, it looked like old times. Later in the game, John had his bell rung and they didn't put him back in, even though he looked and acted okay and had been getting results with the offense earlier.

On defense we held Miami scoreless in the first half, but the Florida heat caved us in, even while we were shutting them out. At the half, Ray May and Ted Hendricks were flushed in the face, and Jerry Logan just flopped onto the locker room floor. The whole defensive line was exhausted, and the offensive line, too. Even if anyone had been inclined to try a pep pill, they wouldn't have done it because they didn't have the pep to go get one.

The temperature was 85 degrees, but on the field in that Orange Bowl it must have been 185. I drank a glass of water with about a pound of salt poured into it, and it helped me to survive the second half. I had felt faint at the end of the second quarter, and I wasn't really sure whether I could keep from passing out. They say being the home team is worth about three points in a game, but under that kind of weather it must be more like ten points. It was that hot for Miami, too, but they were used to it, having played in it all season, practiced in it all week long every week, and trained in it all during the exhibition season. That's a big difference.

We're still a better team than the Dolphins. But we're not better than the Florida heat. After the game I weighed 227, and my eyes were in the back of my head and I had the gaunt look of a ravaged man. I didn't know whether I was going to live or die, and for a few minutes I didn't much care.

Speaking of dying, Ray Perkins almost did. He got creamed and stopped breathing for about twenty seconds. We thought he had broken his neck. He got hit across the field from the Colt bench, and he just lay on the artificial turf without moving. Physicians for both teams ran out to him and treated him frantically. He suffered a head injury in college and he has a steel plate in his head, and that's probably why everyone reacts faster than usual when Ray is down and out cold. It turned out he had a mild concussion, but for a minute they weren't sure which way things were going to go. Today he's fine and we're back to needling him about the steel plate in his head. We tell him he doesn't have to worry—it's the other guy's headache.

I suffered two other losses against Miami—my big toenails. My shoes didn't fit well and they turned up on me at the toes. I began to feel it in the pregame warmups, but I didn't have much choice, so I kept playing with them on. The shoes just worked the nails right off the big toes. After the game I put the nails back in place with a bandage on each until the new ones could grow back in.

Once again, the officials were obnoxious in their calls. I hope this doesn't sound like sour grapes and it shouldn't, because I've made the same charge after games that we won. In the locker room after the game, with a few minutes to regain my strength, I was teeing off on the officiating to Tony Atchison of the *Washington Star*. I said, "They were incompetent and put that in whatever you write." He did, in just those words.

I expected to hear from Rozelle about that one but I never did. His lousy officials have been incompetent ever since the merger of the two pro leagues. Somebody ought to do something about it. Nothing is improved if everyone just continues to shut up about it. The players bitch about it all the time among themselves, and so do the coaches, but nothing seems to come of it. Whatever happened to the almighty press?

On one play, Miami's quarterback, Bob Griese, put his hands under the center to receive the snap. Then he pulled them back, stood up and straightened out the alignment of his backfield. Again he put his hands back under the center. That's a clear violation of the rules. It's an illegal procedure, and it carries a penalty of five yards. I yelled to the closest officials, "What the hell is that?" After we stopped the play for three yards, the ref said, "Well, nothing happened."

I said, "Nothing happened? What kind of baloney is that?"

Once Larry Csonka got tackled and was falling forward. Freddie Miller hit him for us again. Csonka hadn't hit the ground yet, and no whistle had been blown. But we got penalized fifteen yards for what Freddie did. Yet on another play one of the other team's defensive backs pushed our receiver out of bounds and then intercepted the pass. What was the reaction of the officials? Nothing. The play stood.

On two different punts, our guys blocked with their heads in front of the tackler, in accordance with the rules. They were identical blocks, and the films show it. One was called a clip. The other wasn't.

All in one game.

It was ironic that the morning of that game there was a big feature story in the *Washington Post* sports section with the headline:

OFFICIALS OBEY DOUBLE STANDARD: BE ANONYMOUS, BE RIGHT

The story sounded like a paid ad straight out of NFL headquarters. The writer, some guy named Mike Rathet of the Associated Press, said it is "generally accepted that the NFL officials are the best in football."

What kind of a statement is that? They're professionals in a professional league, aren't they? That's like saying the NFL players are the best in football, better than high school or college players. I should hope so.

The article said that not losing their composure is what makes good officials, yet one official last season told Ted Hendricks to go to hell. The story said that instant replays show officials "are almost invariably correct." How often is invariably? Ninety-nine per cent of the time? Or only 50 per cent?

And speaking of instant replays, how about the one at the end of our win over the Rams, when every viewer in the country saw Matt Maslowski catch a "touchdown" pass with one foot clearly out of bounds? The officials were not "invariably" correct on that instant replay.

I told Bill Curry, my roommate, that I wanted to get out of the Players' Association. He tried to talk me out of it because he is a strong believer in the Association. But I still wanted out. I admitted to Bill that while I thought there were still some inequities in the conditions under which the players must work, I was generally satisfied with my lot. The Colts have treated me well, and Carroll Rosenbloom treated me well. He has also treated a lot of other guys well and has gone far out of his way to help many of them prepare for the day when they hang up their cleats, or whatever we're supposed to hang up when we quit playing football for a living. He's staked a lot of them to a start, including Gino Marchetti. Gino's fast-food restaurants now dot the maps of Maryland, Virginia,

Pennsylvania and other states. He helped John Unitas and Bobby Boyd get their restaurant started. He has helped others as well, including Jim Parker, Alex Sandusky and Willie Richardson. And last year he helped me in my planning for a restaurant.

About Carroll Rosenbloom. In his book Bernie Parrish lists Rosenbloom as one of the owners he would like to drive out of pro football. Some facts are in order.

For our pre-season games in 1971, Rosenbloom donated 30,000 tickets to hospitals, schools, orphanages and schools for retarded children in the Baltimore area. Maybe there were a lot of empty seats for our home exhibitions, but Rosenbloom didn't have to give free tickets to anyone. He gave them away for regular season games, too.

Every year he gives $5,000 to help finance five boys' football leagues. Over the years he has spent hundreds of thousands of dollars through the Baltimore Colt Foundation, which he established to finance college educations for Baltimore youths who could not afford college.

Rosenbloom has given the Baltimore Police Boys Clubs over half a million dollars from intrasquad games played by the Colts over the past ten years.

Remember that awful plane crash a few years ago in which all those players from Marshall University and Wichita State were killed? Carroll Rosenbloom gave each school $50,000.

Neither Rosenbloom nor pro football can be too terrible when you consider the people who have been with him at our games. People like Robert Kennedy, Ted Kennedy, Buddy Hackett, Danny Kaye, Richard Nixon, Bob Hope, Paul Newman and Earl Warren. And when Jacqueline Kennedy Onassis attended our game with the Jets in New York last season, she was there as Carroll Rosenbloom's guest.

These days there's a lot of talk—too much of it—about player strikes. You hear it about football and you hear it about baseball. I think it's ridiculous that you hear it at all.

We had a football players' strike in 1970 before the start of training in July. The Players' Association had been in prolonged negotiation with the owners concerning our pension plan. The players were saying they wanted the owners' contributions to our pension plan raised from $2.8 million a year to $6.5 million. They got $4.5 million each year for the next four years, plus another million in insurance benefits.

John Mackey was the leader of the strike. Bill Curry was another of the leading forces in the decision to strike. Now I like and respect both John and Bill. I just happen to disagree with them on this strike business. I know there are some conditions that could stand correcting. We play too damn many exhibition games, for one thing. The officials are hurting the games with too many lousy calls, for another. And third, artificial turf is becoming a danger to our careers.

These are conditions that should be corrected. But go out on strike? Nothing in the life of a pro football player today justifies a strike, and I daresay the same thing goes for baseball. That's why I was a strikebreaker in 1970. In the final few days before training was to start in July, the player representatives were hot on the phone calling their teammates and pleading with them not to report to camp. Bill Curry called me. He told me all the reasons for striking, but I told him I had to disagree with him, that nothing in football justified the extreme action of a strike. So I reported to camp, and I found myself alone.

I walked into the dining room at Westminster College where we trained in the rolling farmland of central Maryland in beautiful and green Carroll County. People in that county make their living as farmers and workers and owners of small businesses, and I bet damn few of them ever went out on strike. So there I was, the only veteran in the training camp of the Baltimore Colts. Only the rookies were there. I sat down and ate my meal alone. Then I went out and practiced. As far as I was concerned that was the thing to do, so I did it.

I knew I would catch a lot of heat for doing it, and I did—with abusive letters and phone calls. I've been called a no-good strikebreaker and a lousy scab. I still get it, two years later.

I think strikes in general have lost their effectiveness. They had their place in the 1930s when Walter Reuther was fighting for the five-day week for his United Auto Workers. And they were effective in events like his sit-down at the Ford plant in Michigan. But today it's a totally different world. And as far as strikes by pro ball players are concerned, I think the whole picture is as funny as it is serious. Somehow I doubt that the American public can work up much sympathy for a twenty-seven-year-old running back or second baseman who makes $45,000 a year for seven months' work, is blessed with the most generous pension plan in the world, sees the country free, flies in plush jet airplanes and stays at posh hotels and gets paid to play ball. And these guys are going out on strike? Man, that's as crazy as the idea that the fans will support them. Yet that's what a lot of players think.

I can just picture Hank Aaron, making $200,000 a

year, or Joe Namath, with $400,000 in the bank just for signing his first contract, going on strike against their employers. I can't stop shaking my head at that silly prospect.

Pro athletes have a tendency to lose their sense of values at times. Obviously, not all of them agree with me, and it may be that hardly any of them do. I just can't see how you can justify being blessed with everything a pro football player or a major league baseball player has and still seriously consider a strike against the owners. Those conditions that do need to be corrected are only minor inconveniences when weighed against the good life we lead.

But there is talk of a strike anyhow—and you hear it about both football and baseball. I just can't see it, and I sure as hell can't imagine the players winning any support from the fans—the people who pay our salaries and make the good life possible for us and finance our pension plan. I'll tell you this right now: If the Players' Association calls another strike, I'll call a press conference immediately and have some things to say. I hope it doesn't come to that, but if it does I'll be *forced* to speak out. And after the press conference you'll know where to find me—on the football field. That's where I was for all three weeks of the strike in 1970, in the training camp of the Baltimore Colts, living up to the contract I had signed with them. That's where all of us should be—playing ball and thanking our lucky stars for what we have, not sticking a gun in the backs of the owners.

Another major factor in my desire to quit the Players' Association is my conviction that unions have outlived their usefulness in this country, at least in their present form and under this present leadership. I don't know who George Meany thinks he is, but I'm not going to let an overweight, cigar-chewing union boss play with my future. As a matter of pride, I'm sure as hell not going to walk around thinking a man like that represents me.

George Meany acts as if he doesn't give a damn for the people of this country, and that's a weird attitude for a man supposedly concerned with helping the workers. He threw his vulgar insults against President Nixon at the AFL-CIO convention in Miami while we were there to play the Dolphins. Now you don't have to love the incumbent President, and a lot of Americans don't love Richard Nixon. A lot of them didn't love Lyndon Johnson either, but Meany and his henchmen didn't thumb their noses at him in a public display the way they did at President Nixon.

Meany gaveled the meeting back to order after the President spoke, and he barely allowed a polite period of time for Nixon to listen to whatever applause King George was willing to permit. He sat him at the lower tier of the head table, a public and stinging rebuff, and the band didn't even play "Hail to the Chief," the musical salute traditionally accorded to the President.

Meany thinks because he controls 13.6 million workers that he's running the whole country, and he figures what's good for Meany is good for the nation. Well, he doesn't control me.

I didn't enjoy telling these things to Bill Curry, but it's something I just had to do. Bill is a class guy and he respects my opinions and my actions, even though he disagrees with me completely on this question. We didn't even argue about it, which is not surprising, because we never argued about anything in the four years we roomed together, since I was a second-year man trying to make it as an outside linebacker and he was trying to win a job after being traded to the Colts from the Green Bay Packers and Vince Lombardi.

Bill is intelligent, articulate, concerned about a lot of things and a lot of people. But he doesn't push his beliefs off on anyone. However, he did tell me after the season that he was requesting a change in roommates. So after four years we got a divorce. There was no community property involved.

One guy I *would* argue with is Bernie Parrish, who gets into these labor questions and others in his book, *They Call It a Game,* which came out last year. It's difficult to be understanding and tolerant with Parrish when his rhetoric is so militant and his arguments so leaky.

Parrish, who calls himself a revolutionary, says this in the second paragraph of the preface to his book: "This book is intended to drive Pete Rozelle, Arthur Modell, Carroll Rosenbloom, Tex Schramm, Clint Murchison, Lou Spadia and the other so-called sportsmen-owners out of professional football. They are my enemies and they know it."

Now that's a nice snappy opening, but it also tells you something about the author: He's at war with the establishment and is intent on destroying the people associated with it. Maybe you agree with that, maybe you don't, but that's what he's saying at the beginning of his preface.

Nor are the owners the only ones to feel the Parrish poison pen. He takes on the coaches, too, with the statement they belong to a society of their own more than they belong to their own teams. He accuses the writers of dishonesty for catering to the league and to the owners, saying that no writer will ever dare criticize. I don't know what papers he reads, but they sure as hell criticize in Baltimore. And over in Washington, a club owner who was one of the absolute powers in the NFL, George Marshall, sued Shirley Povich for $200,000. I gather Povich wrote something Marshall didn't like. That's being afraid to criticize?

Those critics of pro football who bemoan the slave wages that we football players earn never mention playoff bonuses, personal appearance fees, side income from television commercials and shows—and the chance to sell a book knocking it all.

They charge the owners with boosting the values of their franchises while salaries lag behind. Yet the case they cite is the range from $550,000 paid for the Dallas Cowboys in 1960 to the 16 million put up for the Philadelphia Eagles in 1968. What they don't bother to point out is that in 1960 the Dallas Cowboys were an expansion team, with the lowest market value of any franchise. You couldn't have bought any other team in pro football in 1960 for the half-million dollars paid for the Cowboys.

At the other end of that yardstick, it was common knowledge in 1968 when the Eagles were sold for 16 million dollars that the new owners had been taken to the cleaners. The price was not typical, and everyone in pro football was astonished that a sucker could be found for the Eagles at that sum. It was not a representative value for a franchise then or now, and neither was the figure for Dallas in 1960, yet these are the extremes used by the critics to point out the alleged boosting of pro football franchise values. If you have to use extremes to prove a point, it seems to me you don't have a point.

Critics say salaries aren't growing half as fast as the value of those franchises. They talk as if players are still making what they always did. I'm not. Neither is anyone else. What about a guy like John Unitas? He's making $125,-000 now. I'll bet his salary has increased. He surely wasn't always making that much. And what about Fran Tarkenton, Sonny Jurgensen and some of the recent retirees like Jim Brown and Paul Hornung?

Football's critics—those guys who made a lot of money from the game and then made some more by criticizing it —have their own proposals to reform pro football. Wait a minute. Who's calling for a reform of pro football? Bernie Parrish? Dave Meggyesy? Johnny Sample? That's three people right there—out of 208 million.

One suggestion you hear is for public corporations to operate the franchises in pro football. The presumption is that the mere substitution of public corporations for private corporations would somehow automatically make the public operations responsive to the public. I don't know how that would necessarily follow. There's such a thing as unresponsive public corporations, too.

One of Parrish's proposals calls for the payment of "premiums" for those players in "more demanding positions, like quarterback and cornerback." Guess what position Parrish played—cornerback. As for quarterbacks, I thought they already are paid a premium. But wait, Parrish doesn't stop there. He would tie these premiums to specific standards of performance. But how do you do that? Suppose Unitas has a year when he's right on the button with his passes all season long, but he's got a poor set of receivers, or his offensive line doesn't give him any protection, so he doesn't meet the standards set forth. Do you penalize *him?* And if a player is paid only for what he does this year, what about a superstar's contributions over many years? You mean Unitas and Jurgensen in football and Willie Mays in baseball wouldn't be paid for past contributions to their sport? And these proposals would help the players?

These suggestions are socialism, and I think it's accurate to say—whether you agree with them or not—that the American people do not want socialism. Not in their government, and certainly not in their sports.

So much for the flimsy evidence in the indictment against pro football.

Case dismissed.

Chapter 11

Thanksgiving weekend, gave us plenty to be thankful for. Like a smashing 37–14 win over Oakland in which everyone played superb football. Our defense—my favorite topic—held the Raiders to minus one yard passing in the first half, and we wound up intercepting six passes—against the highest scoring team in pro football. Jerry Logan grabbed two and Rick Volk, Tom Nowatzke, Billy Newsome and I got the other four.

Our first-string defense played only a minute and a half in the first quarter. That's how much our offense dominated things with our running game. We played two series, three plays each, in that period. And when the offense wasn't dominating things, the defense was. The Raiders didn't even get a first down in the whole first half.

As for the offense, one headline said it all:

UNITAS OLD SELF IN COLTS' VICTORY

On the plane flying out I noticed Unitas studying his play book and I knew the Raiders were in for it. It seemed like old times. We took a dozen old Colts out with us, including Artie Donovan, Jim Mutscheler and George Prease, John's former teammates. No, Unitas was not going to let *them* down. I began to feel better.

I was making some good plays and feeling strong and I threw their runners for a loss on a couple of sweeps and draws. Once I ran into Gene Upshaw, their left guard, and gave him a shot with my forearm and he asked, "What the hell you got in that damn arm?"

I told him, "Nothing. Just fiber glass."

He looked at me with a frown and said, "You sure of that?"

Early in the game I almost got into a fight on the field with Jimmy Bailey, one of our defensive linemen. I told him to move over and play more toward the middle of the line, the way that defensive formation was designed, but he wouldn't do it. So I pulled him over into position. After the play he said, "Don't do that."

I said, "Listen, if you don't move over to where you should be, I'll kick you out of the damn game. And if you don't like it, you can do something about it."

He apologized. He patted me on the rump and said he was sorry. But he didn't have to apologize. I liked it when he barked at me because I like a player who is fired up like that during the game. When he snapped back at me, I didn't mind it a bit. I was glad to see it.

Marty tells me that when that was happening, one of the TV announcers said, "There's Curtis manhandling one of the Colts' linemen." I'm disappointed he didn't call me an animal—or at least a mad dog.

The season was now eleven games old, and—as always—I evaluated my performance. I had a good game against the Jets in the opener. I broke my thumb against the Browns in the first quarter of the second game and sat out the third game. I was supposed to miss another game or two, but I came back the next week against Buffalo and was named AP Defensive Player of the Week. I played well the following weeks against the Giants and Minnesota. Against Pittsburgh in our seventh game I got into cast trouble and missed those two plays against Bradshaw and Fuqua. I played OK against the Rams in our second Monday night game and made the big play in forcing the fumble which Hendricks took in for the TD. I was pleased with my performance in our second Jets game. I thought I played well against the Dolphins and I know I played a good game, along with everyone else, against Oakland. So after eleven games, maybe I was having a better season than I thought.

But I can never be sure, and that's one of the things that keeps driving me. One of the disadvantages about being determined to be absolutely the best is that you're constantly discontent with your own performance. I can remember only the last few years of Ted Williams as a player, but I know he always took more batting practice than anyone else, including the .250 hitters. Some day I hope to be considered the best damn linebacker in pro football, and maybe the best ever. That's what I want: I want people to say Mike Curtis is the best, better than Dick Butkus, better than Willie Lanier, better than Sam Huff was with his friends in the New York press. Better than anyone.

No wonder I don't sleep well.

After the Oakland game I took a side trip to Los Angeles to film a one-hour TV special called "The Second Super Comedy Bowl," which was to be telecast nationwide on CBS the week before the Super Bowl. Ray May, Bubba Smith and I were on it from the Colts, and we had a whole slew of other ballplayers for company—Dick Butkus, Deacon Jones, Bob Hayes, Roman Gabriel, John Hadl, Marlin Olson and two Redskins from down at the other end of the Baltimore-Washington Parkway, Mike Bass and Brig Owens.

And if we were supposed to be star football players, the lineup of star entertainers was just as good—Rowan and Martin, Jack Lemmon, George C. Scott, Jill St. John, Paul Newman, Walter Matthau, Tony Curtis and Arte Johnson. We were joined by some announcer named Cosell.

Ray, Bubba and I taped several silly skits. I'm amazed at how ballplayers are asked to make jerks of themselves before national TV audiences, but it pays well. The skits called for us to ride bikes and sing and act even more stupid than usual. I did one in a locker room, dressed only in a towel and with shaving cream all over my face.

Before we started taping, the wardrobe man was fitting me and I wondered whether I would look all right on TV with my fair skin. He said, "Oh, you have a beautiful body. You have nothing to worry about." I decided I didn't need anything else from him.

That's a flaky place, that Los Angeles. While we were taping the show, the writer was standing in the back laughing like hell at his own material, but no one else was. We taped the program without an audience, so I guess they'll dub in one of those awful laugh tracks. The dancers showed up looking like a bunch of dogs, but after make-up—presto!—every one a princess. I guess that's why I don't like Los Angeles. Everything is so contrived, so manufactured. Nothing is really what you think it is. That just goes against my whole nature, I guess. I don't blame them or criticize them, and I know it has to be that way in the entertainment world. I've just never liked things—or people—that are not what they are made out to be.

Ray May and I flew back across the country all night, busting a gut to get back in time for Tuesday's films and practice. We picked up a tail wind flying cross-country and made it from Los Angeles to Baltimore in three hours and fifty minutes. We landed at 6 A.M., just in time to go home, eat and get ready to go right back out to practice. So we show up in time and feel we did our conscientious best and then we hear Don McCafferty tell the team, "Bubba's been excused. He has business in Los Angeles."

We knew what the business was—we just didn't know her name.

The critics of football keep harping about their strength as individuals against the establishment. Hell, they're no more individualistic than anyone else. They're group men. Now they're just with a different group, that's all. They wear long hair like the rest of their group and they use four-letter words at every opportunity because "that's telling it like it is"—and they even use that cliché. They seem to deal in clichés all through their books, and all through their thoughts.

Hell, I wear long hair, too—not as long as some, but long. And I read the liberal *Washington Post* every day and I read the liberal *Newsweek* magazine every week. But I can still think for myself and be myself. I don't have to join any group just to hang on.

In his book Meggyesy says he can't separate the game from its rewards—fame and fortune. Come on, now. The desire for recognition is a motivational factor in life itself. What's so unreal about that desire? On the contrary, it is an absolutely natural desire, and if you're totally lacking it, maybe you have a problem. The lowest sales clerk in a store or a typist in an office needs approval. Even my dog does. Maybe the loud voices on the Left should stop their screaming long enough to read a famous work by one of their Leftist colleagues—Dr. Spock's baby book. It's all explained right there.

Football's critics emphasize revolution in their books. We saw some examples of revolution last year in the attempts to stop the government and in the bombing of the U. S. Capitol building. Yet Bobby Kennedy, who was so prominently identified with the Left, used to say we are a nation of laws and not of men. He said it when he was the Attorney General, the nation's chief law enforcement officer, the top law-and-order man in the country.

Let's talk about revolution for a minute. The revolutionaries tell us how dehumanizing football is. What's more dehumanizing than the tactics of the revolutionaries

—like depriving someone of his civil right to go to work by blocking the streets into Washington? Or trying to take over a government building? They talk about the tragic killings in Viet Nam and no one will disagree with that, but then they try to blow up the Capitol and run the risk of killing a lot of people while doing it. What's more dehumanizing than that?

And while they were trying to stop the government in Washington from operating, they kept a lot of hourly-paid people like household domestics and laborers from getting to their jobs and from getting paid for that day. What's more dehumanizing than that? Yet the revolutionaries who want to revolutionize football and everything else are the ones who did all those things.

If it's good for your cause that makes it OK. That's their attitude. It was also the attitude of Karl Marx. He said the same thing in the Communist Manifesto—the end justifies the means.

You hear from the same sources—including ex-player authors—that there are racial problems in football. They should limit their talk to what they've experienced. I'll tell you what I've experienced.

We have three interracial marriages on the Colts—Eddie Hinton, John Williams and Ronnie Gardin. They are all accepted by everyone else on the team. They mingle socially and go to church with others and do everything else with the rest of the Colts in our social life. Two of my best friends on the Colts are Bubba Smith and Ray May, both black.

The cliché criticism that there aren't any black quarterbacks in pro football is both misleading and just plain wrong, which seems to be characteristic of too damn many protests in these protest-filled times. In the first place, there *are* black quarterbacks in the National Football League. I know, because we have one. He's Karl Douglas, a rookie last year and a fine football prospect. The Buffalo Bills have a black quarterback in Jim Harris.

That's two and maybe two isn't a hundred, but it's two more than there used to be, and obviously there is no barrier in pro football that would keep that two from growing to twenty-two. It just depends on what's coming out of the pipeline from the colleges.

Douglas shows promise of making it as a first-rate pro quarterback. He's a good passer and displays a lot of enthusiasm. The offensive linemen tell me he's smart and shows a potential for leadership and they say they enjoy playing for him. The Colts obviously have high regard for Douglas—they made him one of their top draft choices. Any fan can tell you that a team's top draft choices are among its most valuable business assets each year and are not spent lightly. Tremendous time and intelligence go into the selection of top draft choices, and a team considers their selection a major investment. The decision is made on the basis of the team's present or future needs and the ability of the player in question to meet that need. I've never heard of any team asking what color a top draft choice is. Including the Colts when they went for Douglas.

Douglas will make it as a pro quarterback when he masters the defenses. The offensive players say that's all he needs. That takes several years, but time is on his side.

That brings us to an equally important aspect of the race question. The charge is sometimes made that black players who were quarterbacks in college are switched to another position in the pros and so this is racial prejudice. No, it isn't. It's the difference between playing in an amateur league and playing as a professional, with and against the best players in the world.

Hell, many a ballplayer has been switched in the pros. The standards are much higher because the caliber of the players is much higher. You have to be stronger and faster and smarter and more experienced and tougher and better than you ever imagined in college. Maybe you were fast enough in college to be a wide receiver, but in the pros you don't quite measure up to the higher speed requirements, so they make you a tight end. What's so awful about that? They're putting you where they think you'll do best. You can always be left to play your old college position—and head for home after the first squad cut in your one and only season as a pro football player. Or you can take the advice of men who know a lot more than you do and move to the position they suggest and go on to a successful and highly rewarding career.

We have a guy on our team who came up as a quarterback and got switched to wide receiver. Sam Havrilak. He's white.

Hell, it happened to me. I played fullback and linebacker at Duke and was drafted as a linebacker. In 1965, first season, I played behind Tony Lorick and Jerry Hill at running back, which is to say I didn't play much. The next season they moved me to outside linebacker.

But I didn't yell foul. A fullback has a shot at a lot more money and fame than a linebacker and I was aware of this. But I figured Don Shula knows what he's talking about because he's a lot older and been around a lot and has produced champions, so who am I, twenty-three years old and one year out of college, to argue against a man so respected and so successful in his profession? So I made the switch, and sure enough, Don Shula knew what he was talking about. I'm making good money and I'm playing first-string and everything's coming up roses, all because Shula knew what was best for me and I believed him.

A clear part of the argument about black quarterbacks is the strong implication that because there aren't X number of black quarterbacks it means blacks are the victims of economic prejudice. But that's wrong, too. Let me tell you why.

Quarterbacks aren't the only ones who make a lot of money in this business. Running backs and wide receivers make a potful, too, and many of them outearn a lot of the quarterbacks. Guys like Paul Warfield, Bob Hayes, Otis Taylor, Duane Thomas, Gale Sayers, O. J. Simpson, Charley Taylor, Larry Brown, Leroy Kelly, Matt Snell, Emerson Boozer, Floyd Little, Mike Garrett. They're all black.

Ebony magazine makes the point well in its November, 1971, issue. It shows there are 387 black players in professional football. That's out of 1,040 players, a ratio of one out of three. *Ebony* also shows fifty-six black wide receivers and eighty black running backs. That's a lot of guys making a lot of money. Not much economic discrimination there.

It's a sorry note that we even have to talk about this. Color never was that big a thing with me. And it isn't with most other players or owners. Those figures compiled from *Ebony* show that. I don't think of a guy as a black quarterback or a black wide receiver anyhow. I just think of him as a ballplayer. Period.

Chapter *12*

When you play the Buffalo Bills, the outcome isn't always the most interesting aspect of the game. This game was a case in point. Another shutout, 24–0. The first time it was 43–0. That's a combined score of 67–0. See what I mean?

The interesting part was the combat on the field. Not the game, the combat. I was aware all day that I might get a shot at that guy Reilly, their lineman who took a cheap shot at me in our first game of the year. But the opportunity never came. I'll get him this year. I won't forget. One guy I did get a chance at was Donnie Green. I got kicked out of the game for it, but what the hell.

Green gave Rick Volk a clothesline shot and Volk called

him some names. Green clubbed him in the mouth. We were expecting something like that. . . . Volk had had trouble with the Bills the year before. At that time Rick had intercepted a pass, and Paul Costa ran all the way downfield and gave Rick a cheap shot in the back of the helmet with his forearm. The ref said he hadn't seen it, of course. Rick and Costa all alone in the end zone, the rest of us down at the other end of the field, and the ref doesn't see it.

Several of us remembered this and were prepared for any eventuality. When Green took that cheap shot at Rick, the players started to scuffle and gather around. I vaulted over the circle of players, landed in the middle and swatted Green across the forehead with my arm. It was a right —a right to the face mask.

Ted Hendricks had better luck. He came right after me and got Green in the back—just where Costa had gotten Rick last year. Green went down from the blow, and that was all we wanted. It all broke up after that. Nobody hurt. No permanent damage done. We were just making a point.

But the three of us—Hendricks, Green and I—got thrown out. And what penalty was called for all that? Unsportsmanlike conduct against the Colts. Unsportsmanlike conduct against the Bills. Offsetting penalties. Neither team gets penalized any yardage. That's a farce and the players know it. You can start a war and never get penalized because the other team will retaliate and the refs will say both teams were at fault and since both teams would normally get penalized, the penalties offset each other. Who said two wrongs don't make a right?

It was the third time I'd been thrown out in my pro career. Undoubtedly, I would hear from Rozelle. I knew that from experience. It would cost me $150 because I was on the field when it happened. If you come off the bench, that's 200 bucks. On the field, the rates are cheaper.

What really would happen was that technically I'd be put on probation. If you're a good boy, you get your money back anyhow.

Ah, the feuds that dehumanize the game of football.

O. J. Simpson once said that Nick Buoniconti of Miami is more of a thinking man's middle linebacker than I am, that I'm just an animal. Man, that's not even original. That kind of talk helps the old animal image, but isn't there such a thing as a thinking man's animal? I was thinking about that remark by O. J. once when I made the tackle on him. I put a little extra mustard on it and as he was getting up he said, "Way to hit, big fella." I didn't feel the need to say anything.

Could be that the Colts have picked up some support in the feud with the city over conditions at Memorial Stadium. The Bills were complaining about their dressing room facilities. What's wrong with the facilities now? Roaches. Buffalo players were saying there were roaches in the dressing room. Now *that's* what I call dehumanizing. O. J. Simpson said he had them in his shoes, and the way he said it gave me the impression he didn't care for the arrangement. Funny thing, though, we've never noticed any roaches in the home team dressing room. I guess if the maintenance crew sees any roaches around the Colts' room they just shoo them over to the visitors' quarters. You can't ask for more loyalty than that.

When we saw the films of the Miami-New England game, one play leaped off the screen and stuck with me.

144

It went like this: The Patriots intercept a pass from Bob Griese. Griese starts toward the man with the ball. He sees a blocker enter his path. Griese turns and goes away. If he had slowed the guy up, the guys behind the play could have caught up with the defender and tackled him. Instead he went for a touchdown. It tells a defensive player something about a quarterback. Sonny Jurgensen got hurt making that same play for the Redskins this year—in an exhibition game, no less. But he stopped the guy.

Somebody asked Sonny why he had tackled the interceptor and Jurgy gave a classic answer: "I thought that was the purpose of the game." To Sonny it was basic. Ditto here.

I had an encounter with Bubba Smith before this game. At practice one day he said, "Hey, Curtis. Let's you and me go one on one."

So I lined up and hit him hard as I made my charge across the imaginary line of scrimmage.

Then he made his charge and bumped me in the chest.

Then I said, "Okay, my turn again."

But Bubba says, "Naw. You don't want to do that anymore."

Then in the dressing room we were talking about that TV show we filmed in Los Angeles. Bubba heard I got a thousand bucks for my part of the show, because I agreed to pose dressed only in that towel. It's regarded as a semi-nude scene or something, and it turns out there's a premium for that kind of performance. So I got the thousand while the others got 250.

Now Bubba didn't know that I knew that he got only 250. So I asked him how much he got, and Bubba said, "I got twenty-five hundred." Hell, he wasn't even willing to make me think he got what I did. He had to top me by fifteen hundred.

The price of being a well-known athlete is often steep. When Bill Kilmer, the Redskins' quarterback, was arrested one Washington newspaper made it the top story of the day and spread it across page one, that same week when we were getting ready for Miami. At the very least you would have thought he was guilty of some heinous crime. Know what the charge was? Disorderly conduct!

On a day when India and Pakistan were in the first hours of a real shooting war which threatened to engulf the Soviet Union and the United States and everyone else, one Washington paper devoted its top headline on page one to Kilmer's arrest. For disorderly conduct.

In the Washington area there must be a hundred people a night arrested for disorderly conduct. Ever heard about any of them? I'm not complaining about the good life ballplayers have, but that Kilmer incident is an example of some of the things you have to put up with.

Roy Lester, my high school coach, got it that same week. Roy Lester is a class guy. He's a good head of a nice family and he's a good builder of men. He took me and many others by the scruff of the neck and made football players out of us and taught us discipline and respect and fairness. Then he went to the University of Maryland because they told him they needed him. But they put handcuffs on him and then, before the players he recruited for Maryland had a chance to develop, the university administration fired Roy Lester. A lot of students are poorer, and so are their parents. If ever there was a bum rap, Roy got it. But he'll come out ahead. At least his ulcer will calm down—after he finishes hurting inside.

I'm sorry Roy got the axe. Not surprised, just sorry. He wanted a disciplined team, and you can't have a disciplined football team at Maryland University right now. They keep yearning there for the football days of wine and roses of the Jim Tatum era. What the hell do they think Tatum was, a child psychiatrist? He was a damn tough disciplinarian who would knock the block off any of his players who got out of line, and they knew it. That's one reason they won. And the reverse is one reason why today's Terps lose.

I'm sorry about Roy, real sorry. But I'm even sorrier about what his firing represents—another victory for permissiveness, for student demonstrations and for ignoring the coach and what he tells you to do. What the hell, he's only the coach. Never mind what your father and mother tell you, either. They're only your parents. Never mind what anyone tells you to do. Do what you want to do, man. Do your own thing. Trot out all those instant clichés and never mind about living in a structured society. It's every man for himself, and never mind what Bobby Kennedy said about our being a nation of laws and not of men. Forget all that stuff. It doesn't mean a thing. It's just red-white-and-blue garbage.

That's really what upsets me about Roy Lester's firing. I know what Roy Lester had to deal with.

Ballplayers get to see a lot of society, maybe a lot more than some of our editorial writers. We see a lot of students and we're with them in their school atmosphere, not talking in a sterile television studio. We see them in their tee shirts and blue jeans. We walk through their parking lots and down their hallways and see them in their classrooms and their assemblies. And I don't like everything I see.

Back home in my native Montgomery County, I'm regarded by some people as a real right-winger. Sure I'm a conservative, and I think this country could use a healthy shot of conservatism for a few years, but that kind of thinking doesn't mean I'm a redneck or a Wallace supporter. It just means I see a lot of things which I consider wrong in today's society, wrong and unhealthy—and I think the reason usually is permissiveness or ultraliberalism or whatever term you prefer.

Hell, permissiveness is a word you never even heard when I was in high school or college. Now you not only hear it, you see it. I see it every time I go into a high school. I know the students can get their grass in the hallways of their school in some areas of Montgomery County. I've been interrupted while speaking to a high school assembly by a student who walks up to me and asks for my autograph—right in the middle of my speech. He didn't get it either.

I've spoken in schools where some students were lying on the floor—just stretched out as if their high school auditorium were a beach or a park bench. When I asked the principal why they were allowed to lie on the floor, I was told it is an experimental school and kids are encouraged to do what they want. You know, do your own thing. That's the cliché that means don't worry about right or wrong.

A typical example of the sort of thing that upsets me so about the conditions in our schools: A kid exploded a firecracker while I was visiting a school. I asked the principal what he would do with the kid—they had him in the office—and he said they probably wouldn't do anything.

He asked me what I would do and I said, "I'd expel his fanny in a minute."

I learned from some of the parents later that they were not asked about the decision to run that whole junior high school on an experimental basis. It's just run that way, and if your kid is a student there and you don't agree with a lawless school, that's tough. One father told me he asked at a parents' meeting if school authorities knew what the effects would be on those students when they leave that ungoverned junior high school and move on to high school—and a return to the real world of discipline. The answer was no, they couldn't really tell you what might happen to the child at that point.

I can't believe that kind of thinking, but there it is—and I've seen its results. It's conditions like these that make me think I might run for election to the County School Board when my football career is over and I move back to Montgomery County. I can see now what forces people into public service. At times conditions just seem so bad that you feel you have to get into the battle and try to help straighten things out. Maybe that's what I'll do.

I don't think I would enjoy public life—running for office, making speeches and putting up with a lot of guff—but maybe that's a small price to pay if you can help put your society back on an even keel.

I don't have to wait to serve on the school board before I can make some contributions to improving our society. I think pro ballplayers should spend time and energy contributing to society while they are active and have the ability to help deserving causes through the use of their name and their support.

We do—football players individually and pro football collectively. That's why I serve on the board of directors of the YMCA in the part of Montgomery County, Maryland, where I grew up. From where I live now, it's an hour and a half's drive to a meeting. And if I can help publicize their causes, I'm glad to do it. The same thing goes for the high school speeches I give, and I give a lot of them. An hour and a half over, and an hour and a half back. I may be at the school only an hour, but I've spent four hours in all.

And when I'm talking to those Montgomery County students, I do it free, just as many other football players do. I'm at the point in my career where I get $800 a speech, plus expenses. But I waive that fee when I'm speaking to those students in my old community.

I'm not complaining. It's the least I can do right now. And when I retire as a player, I'll have the time to do more.

I'm only one example. Almost every pro football player does this kind of thing, and some do a lot more. They do it on their own because they are concerned citizens, and sometimes they render a particular service in response to a program begun by the National Football League itself. Two examples of NFL projects which people should know about involve drug abuse and Viet Nam.

The NFL staged a real blitz on drug abuse which I don't have to describe in detail, because if you saw even one pro football game on television this season you know what I mean. A long parade of players made statements warning against the dangers of drugs. They asked me to tape one of the messages, but the only time they could set it up was just minutes before our game with the Vikings and I couldn't make it.

The U. S. Department of Health, Education, and Welfare sent a letter to the NFL thanking pro football for "the talent, time and resources you have contributed in producing and showing the drug abuse spots during NFL games." HEW said the messages by the players "had significant impact in our overall attempts to provide the public with a source of accurate and helpful information on drugs and their misuse."

President Nixon praised the NFL contributions, too, plus the efforts of collegiate athletes. The President said, "I know of no program that has paid off more, that has been more effective than what the athletes of America have done."

And in case you're wondering, all the players did it free.

The President made one particularly good point, a point which most athletes recognize. It's one of the basic reasons we devote our time and energy to worthy public causes. The President was speaking about getting through to young people and he said, "A politician can't reach them. A teacher can't reach them. You can, because they admire you." He must be right. The messages resulted in more than 100,000 written requests for more information about drugs. I like to think pro football did some real good on that problem.

It's not unusual to read about football players touring Viet Nam, and that in itself is evidence of the contributions by many players to help our guys over there. I was supposed to go on the last one, but I was getting married and had to pass it up. I hated to miss it, and I hope they ask me again. I'd go in a minute.

Sixteen players are making this trip. It's the seventh straight year that NFL players have done this, on a volunteer basis. And each year more and more players are volunteering to go.

John Unitas made the first trip, in 1966. Bill Curry is going on this one. Two other Colts have done it, too—Billy Ray Smith in 1969 and Tom Matte in 1971.

Unitas isn't the only star ever to go, either. Joe Namath has been to Viet Nam, and so have Bart Starr and Lance Alworth and Greg Landry and Larry Csonka and Floyd Little and Dick Butkus and Tucker Frederickson. Plus one of our most distinguished grads—Jack Kemp, Congressman Kemp. And three former players who are now in television—Don Meredith, Pat Summerall and Frank Gifford.

The sixteen guys making the latest trip bring the total number of pro football players to visit our troops in Viet Nam to seventy-five. That seems worth mentioning.

Chapter *13*

We beat the Dolphins, far and away our biggest win of the year and our most impressive. So that's all the fans were talking about, right? Wrong. They seemed more interested in the fact that I decked a fan who ran onto the field during the game and tried to steal the ball. I didn't think it was that much of a big deal and I still don't. To me the game was the thing. The game is always the thing.

We beat the Dolphins soundly, 14–3, and they were never in it.

John Mackey made a key contribution to our victory, one that doesn't show in the statistics. We had a players-only meeting before the game and he threw a challenge at us, saying there are no great men, only great challenges, and if we met this challenge we would have the right to be called a great team. Bubba Smith said it sounded like what Vince Lombardi would say, and he's right.

We had another Vice Presidential visit in the locker room before the game. Vice President Agnew came over from Washington again. We were dressing and getting ready when six guys came into the room, checking cubby holes and vents and every damn corner. Then the Vice President comes in, with four more guys—Secret Service Agents. Then Governor Mandel comes in, and he's accompanied by two of his own agents. Then Jack Nicklaus, the great golfer, comes in, only he's on his own. I guess that shows we attach more importance to our public officials than we do to our sports stars, at least once in a while. The presence of Nicklaus rekindled the Tampa talk, the rumor being that he would buy the Colts from Rosenbloom and take the team to Tampa. Those birdies must pay better than I thought.

The Vice President said he was sending me a picture of me tackling Roman Gabriel in that 1968 game when I first made Defensive Player of the Week. He wants me to auto-graph it, and when I do I'll merely be returning the favor. When Marty and I got married eight months before, he was kind enough to send us a beautiful large ash tray of Fostoria crystal with the Vice Presidential seal and his autograph cut into the crystal. It must weigh a ton. I thanked him for the wedding gift, then I asked him how come he could take off Saturday. I thought the Vice President was always too busy for that. He said he just wanted to see this game because it was so important.

I had nine tackles and five assists against the Dolphins,

but the only contact anyone remembers is one that didn't count—the one against that fan.

I've seen a lot of fans run onto the field in games on TV and I always said that if it ever happened when I was on the field, I would simply deck the guy. But this fan wasn't satisfied with just making an ass of himself, he wanted to steal something too—the ball.

Our defense was on the field and Miami was coming up to the line of scrimmage. There were about three minutes left in the game. All of a sudden this fan is running up the field. He darts in among the players and scoops up the ball and starts to run away with it. So I decked him. That's all I did. I didn't tackle him, although I could have—and a lot of people said I did. And I didn't slug him, although I felt like it. I knocked him down. Period. Then the officials got the ball and the cops got the fan. And the fan got a night in jail, a visit to the hospital and a loss of $100. He was charged with trespassing and ordered to appear in court. He chose to forfeit the hundred bucks, so he didn't show up in court.

Guess who wound up with the ball. Me. Our equipment manager got it and gave it to me after the game.

Then came the phone calls. Four days later, Marty had to take the phone off the hook. On that fourth day alone we received six calls, three of them long distance, but no one would give a name. I don't know whether they were calling to praise me or condemn me, but they all admitted they wanted to talk to me about the incident. I wasn't home—honest.

I couldn't really believe the reaction. I was getting so many questions I grew tired of the whole thing. I'm still being asked about it. Then, to add to my astonishment, people asked about the possibility of a lawsuit by the fan against me. Can you imagine that? I can't. But damned if that wasn't what some people were wondering about. Here's a man, thirty years old, and old enough to know better, who breaks the law not once but twice—going onto the field and then trying to steal something. And they were saying *he* might sue *me*. My own lawyers and the Colts' attorneys talked to each other and there didn't seem to be anything to worry about, which I was glad to hear because I wasn't worried about anything anyhow. And the Players' Association reminded me that they have attorneys, too, plus an insurance policy carrying $10,000 of liability protection. I told them no, thanks, just refund my $200 in dues.

The people who defended the fan say it was only a football. Hell, it was only $20. If some guy runs up to you and grabs $20, aren't you going to try to stop him? Or even if he tries to take it from the guy next to you?

One story quoted the fan as saying, "I just thought, 'Gee I sure would like the game ball,' and simply decided to go after it. I made up my mind and figured I'd go ahead and do it."

Suppose those other 60,000 fans had decided the same thing? Maybe we could avoid this by just giving away a football to each fan as he enters the stadium before the game. I hate to sound like Archie Bunker, but I just cannot justify in my mind seeing a man break the law twice in front of 60,000 people and millions more on national TV. And everyone just stands around there and lets him do it. In our label-conscious society this brands me as a hard-hat, a right-winger, but to me it's a simple case of right and wrong. You do something wrong, you get punished for it. That's what I was always taught. And what an example that would have been for the youth of our nation—sitting there watching a guy break the law twice while those policemen and six game officials don't do a thing. Things like that make the law-and-order types look like Solomon in all his wisdom.

I just happen to think laws should be obeyed, and so should parents and teachers and coaches. And I think most Americans are reasonable, level-headed people who feel the same way.

The vocal minority from the Left will dispute me on this. To me, though, it's a simple question of whether we are to live in a structured society. If we are—and I think we are—then we're going to need laws by which to govern ourselves. I don't see anything so objectionable or unreasonable in that. And if you don't like a particular law or a particular decision or a particular national policy, then you move to change it. But you don't strengthen any society by defying its laws. When you do that you strike at the very fabric which holds our society together. A society which defies its own laws isn't a society at all, and a nation which defies its own laws isn't a nation at all. It's just a disjointed band of individuals wandering through a fruitless existence.

I don't think Americans want that for our nation, not most of us. I think most Americans feel it is reasonable and sane to live under the law, to elect officials and establish policy through the orderly elective process, and to express dissatisfaction and institute change through the same orderly process. The book called *The Real Majority* confirmed this just a couple of years ago. It proved the political theory that Americans reject the extreme on either side. We prefer the center, and centrist candidates usually win elections for that reason, according to the authors of that book.

I agree with that. I'm not an extremist, and I don't think knocking a guy down when he's trying to steal something makes me one. And I don't think believing in rules and laws and our obedience to them makes me an extremist either. I think it makes me an average American.

People were writing letters. The reaction continued to that incident. I can't believe that so many people would get that excited about something like that, but it happened. People usually write to ask for autographs or pictures or to tell you they like the Colts, or they like you or their son likes you. The fan incident changed all that. Now they were writing to express their views with great feeling on one side or the other. I had been getting about seventy-five letters a week, which put me second or third behind Unitas in fan mail. Then—in one day—I received seventy letters. They came from Texas, New Jersey, Virginia, Florida, Wisconsin, California, Michigan, Rhode Island, Illinois, New York, Connecticut, Missouri—and Baltimore. I even got one from Governor Mandel—a picture of the event, autographed by the Governor. And a letter came from Whittier, California—but not from President Nixon.

It seems most of the letter-writers agreed with me. I'd give you a specific breakdown—for and against—except for one thing: I didn't keep score. I couldn't get that worked up about it. I thought I did something that needed to be done. To me, it was that simple.

There was a nice wire service story that same week

about a visit six of the Colts made to seven children in a pre-Christmas party. It was for children of American men missing in action in Viet Nam or held as prisoners of war by the North Vietnamese. It was part of a program called "No Greater Love," sponsored by an organization known as America's Sports Stars for POWs and MIAs. I wasn't able to make it because I had to give a speech that day. The story said more than 2,000 children would be remembered by sports stars with gifts on Christmas and on their birthdays. So six of our guys went to visit these kids, and our president, Steve Rosenbloom, went with them.

Bill Curry was one of the six, and that shouldn't surprise anyone. Ray May was another. There was even a nice picture in the paper of Bill and Ray down on all fours rolling a football around with a two-year-old boy. When you see a picture of Bill Curry and Ray May doing something like that, you can be sure it's not posed.

For Ray it was the second time this season his good works have found their way into print, but he'd be the last guy in the world to brag about them. Bill Gildea of the *Washington Post* did a long feature story earlier about Ray's work as a bachelor father.

Ray has taken three errant boys under his wing. He's their foster father. They're all in their late teens; Ray is only 25, but he's their father and a good one, too. He spends all his spare time with them, takes them on his trips every time he can and is totally responsible for the boys.

Ray even had a fourth boy, but he had to send him back to the authorities because he couldn't afford to keep him. He spent so much of his own money that he just couldn't afford a fourth boy. He said he could have kept the fourth if he had sold his car, but he needed the transportation for the boys anyhow. And as he says in Gildea's column, "I'm trying like hell to get him back."

Here's a guy who's spending thousands of dollars on three kids who aren't his, giving up virtually all of his free time as a bachelor in his mid-twenties, and guess what he says about all this: "You know, I don't think I sacrificed enough last year. There were some things I had I could have done without. I won't let it happen this year."

So what does Ray May do with his money from our Super Bowl win? He goes out and spends it on a farm for his boys in Kansas, and he spent most of his time this past off-season repairing the farmhouse. And if you don't think by now that Ray May is a great man, listen to this comment by him to Bill Gildea:

"I want to help them broaden their outlook. There's going to be hard work—cutting down trees, mending fences—all things that have to be done together. We're going to have a horse and maybe they can get to appreciate it.

"The big thing is to be always with them. They've never had somebody who was there when they needed him. I want to treat each one like he was mine and I was his."

Ray May's good works remind me of Lenny Lyles, who was an outstanding defensive back with the Colts for twelve years. He was our defensive captain in 1968 and 1969 and it was a pleasure for me to play with him and under his leadership.

Lenny is a product of the ghettos of Louisville, Kentucky. He's back there now and he lives in a 10-room house which is a long way from his boyhood home in more than just miles.

When he was in college at the University of Louisville, one of his best friends and closest teammates was the quarterback. This guy was white, and Lenny is black, but the white guy used to come over to Lenny's house in the ghetto on Sundays for soul food of greens, beef and corn. His name was John Unitas.

Lenny always did a lot of good around Baltimore working with kids, and he's doing it again back in Louisville. He speaks an average of three nights a week to youth groups, plays football with the neighborhood kids and is active with the Urban League, the March of Dimes, the Boy Scouts, the Health and Welfare Council and, well, you name it and he's doing it. No wonder he was named one of the ten outstanding young men in America this year by the U. S. Jaycees.

I've been devoting a chapter to each of our games, but our final game of the regular season isn't worth a chapter. I wouldn't mention it at all, except that it has raised a question that needs to be answered. We lost to New England, 21–17, and some people—probably the writers—have said maybe we lost on purpose so we wouldn't have to play Kansas City in the playoffs. That's so ridiculous it doesn't even deserve a reply, but I'll give one anyhow. In the first place, if Kansas City were as good as these rumor-spreaders seem to think, we would be playing them in the playoffs anyhow. If they were not that good, then we would have no reason to fear them. Who in his right mind would take a dive against the New England Patriots and lose out on all the post-season goodies, not to mention the chance to set a whole slew of records and compile a powerful argument for a fat raise on his next contract?

I suffered another injury in the game, too. Well, not exactly in the game. I got hurt warming up. Not everyone can make that claim. I was bumping pads with one of our tackles, Dennis Nelson, the way you do to loosen up your shoulder muscles. Except that Nelson missed my pads and let me have it right across the bridge of the nose. Which gave me a red scab. I would have gotten sore at Dennis, but he's six feet, five inches tall and he weighs 260 pounds. I'm very patient with guys like that.

Of all the lousy luck, heaped on top of everything else that happened in one day, I had to go to a banquet that evening. That's when you really feel the burden of defeat. You're standing around acting just as pleasant as can be and answering questions until you're blue in the face while everyone else is having one helluva good time eating and drinking and laughing it up. And all this time you're being pulled apart inside. At times like that you wish you could tell the nice people that they can keep your personal appearance fee and you'll just stay home and lock yourself off from the outside world.

The next afternoon I went along with some of the guys to visit Children's Hospital for an hour and a half to talk to the kids over there and try to give them something to smile about at Christmas. We gave out some pictures and signed autographs for these kids and, as I always do, I came away pretty damn sorry for those poor kids and pretty thankful that I've been blessed with everything I have, especially my health. There's no sadder sight to me than a sick child.

Chapter *14*

Christmas came one day late, and the nicest present we received came from some friends in Cleveland. They gave us a New Year's trip to Miami.

We beat the Browns, 20–3, in Cleveland. It must have been pretty boring for those who saw it, because we dominated everything after the first five minutes. In those opening minutes the Browns were moving the ball on us, and I was worried that we would lose the game—and end the season. I chewed out the defensive line and told them to start performing the way they're supposed to or it would be the season for us. I don't know whether that did it, but we toughed it out from then on. The game seemed to turn around and the tide was suddenly flowing in our direction. After that it was no contest.

Bubba Smith was still mad as hell about the New England loss and was taking it out on every Cleveland player who got in his way. He played one helluva game and was a big reason why the momentum continued in our direction. He blocked two field goals. I don't know when I last saw one player block two field goal attempts in the same game—if I ever did. Each time it took more starch out of the Browns and added more to ourselves.

Bubba said some interesting things in the dressing room after the game. He told one reporter, "Hey, man, I'm going to be completely honest with you. We wanted to beat New England, win our division, beat Kansas City and play a championship game at our home field. We're used to being champions. We don't care what people are saying. We just want to get back into the Super Bowl and prove a point. Blooper Bowl, Fluke Bowl—that's what everybody has been saying about last year's game. We just want to prove a point."

So the following Sunday it was the American Football Conference championship game, Baltimore versus Miami. The Dolphins got there by beating Kansas City in pro football's longest day. They went six periods and Miami's kicker, Garo Yepremian, booted a field goal that kicked the Dolphins all the way into the next week. People were wondering if physical exhaustion from playing a game and a half would drain the Dolphins for their game against us. No such luck. They had to be in shape and they had a week to recover. And they played on Christmas Day, the day before us, so they had one day more than we did to rest anyhow. They would be rested and ready, which wasn't the way we would prefer it, but you can't have everything.

Those six periods raised an interesting question, though. What happens if a game is still tied after six periods? Do the teams get another half-time intermission? You couldn't expect them to go right into a seventh period without a rest, especially if the theory is they need an intermission after only two periods. So after six periods do you have a second half time? Presumably provisions have been made for that eventuality. One of the biggest problems, of course, would be for the band. They might have to play "America the Beautiful" a second time.

John Unitas was in Houston the Monday before the Dolphins' game, and what he told their Touchdown Club banquet made the defensive team feel better about the season. He gave the defense the credit for getting the Colts into the AFC championship game. John told them, "The defense has played fantastic all year. The offense has contributed its share but was not as consistent as we wanted. We owe the better part of the season to the defense."

Weeb Ewbank, John's old coach, was there and he agreed. He said, "During the period when Johnny was recuperating and Morrall was not playing as well as he has in some years, it is no question their defense carried them." Coming from the former Colts' coach and the guy who whipped us in the Super Bowl, that sounded just fine.

Our defense was getting more and more attention, and these playoff games with their nationwide TV were helping all the more. People were learning about us and our reputation was growing. I'm positive we are the absolutely best defensive team in professional football, and now more and more fans and writers and broadcasters are saying it. The image grows—with figures to prove it.

The teams for the Pro Bowl were announced that week, and I was picked as one of the middle linebackers for the AFC team, along with Willie Lanier of the Chiefs. It's the third time I've been picked—first as an outside linebacker and now twice as a middle linebacker. The coaches do the voting and no coach is allowed to vote for any of his own players, so that makes you doubly proud when you're selected. I wondered if my cast got any votes. That business about the thumb gave me added satisfaction. I thought back to the Cleveland game in September, and how uncertain things had looked for the team and for me. And there we were in the playoffs, with one win under our belts already, playing in the conference championship game, and I managed to miss only one game with the thumb and got picked for the Pro Bowl, too. Things could have been worse.

Being selected for the Pro Bowl pleases any player, and not just for vanity's sake. It means a lot to his career, to his reputation, to the amount of money he earns. It even helps to determine how long his career will last.

A lot of it depends—I'll say it again—on such factors as how good a game you played when you were on the Monday night TV game; how you looked when your road game was on national TV instead of merely on a regional telecast; how well you played before the New York press, including the wire services reporters, the national sports magazines and any other national outlets.

I must have performed up to someone's standards, thumb or no thumb, or I wouldn't have been picked.

I'll remember the game long after, or at least I'll remember being selected to play in it. I'll remember it at least until the end of 1972, when my current four-year contract runs out and I negotiate a new contract. Then I'll make it a point to remind our general manager, Don Klosterman, that I was picked for the Pro Bowl last year. Maybe I'll be lucky enough to be able to remind him that I was picked for it this year, too.

That's what those negotiating sessions seem to be—reminders. You walk in and they remind you you're not getting any younger and so they can't give you the kind of money they can to a younger player with more years ahead of him. And you remind them you're only twenty-nine or thirty and that's not exactly Social Security age. In fact, you're at the peak of your career physically and you know infinitely more about the game and your instincts are now vastly superior to those of a guy who's been in the league only three or four years instead of seven or eight.

Then they remind you that they can't just pay every player what he wants or they'd go bankrupt. Then you remind them that you're not just any player. You remind them that you've been the A.P. "Defensive Player of the Week" three times, that you've made the Pro Bowl three times, that you've been picked for the All-Pro team and in 1970 you were voted the American Football Conference's "Defensive Player of the Year." Then you remind them that when you signed your four-year contract, you were an outside linebacker and the amount of your salary was based on that position; and the next year you were moved to middle linebacker, a much more responsible position because the whole defense revolves around the middle linebacker's performance. But you didn't ask to renegotiate your contract. Instead, you've played as a satisfied ballplayer all that time.

Then they'll ask me how much I want and I'll tell them $125,000 a year.

There will then be a long silence—or an immediate explosion.

They'll remind me that that's what John Unitas makes, and I'll tell them I know that. And they'll ask me what makes me think I should make what Unitas makes. And I'll remind them that Unitas hasn't made an All-Star team for five years. And I'll remind them that Unitas is the middle of the offense, and I'm the middle of the defense.

Then we'll see whose reminders worked.

For the championship game with the Dolphins, we practiced in Tampa. Guess what we saw when we got off the plane in Tampa? Fifteen thousand people. I still find it hard to believe. Fifteen thousand people went to an airport to greet a team that wasn't even playing a game in their city. We were just there to practice. But they wanted Carroll Rosenbloom to get the message. The message was simply, "Here we are, ready and anxious to greet you and support you in the style to which you would like to become reaccustomed."

One thing bothered me about our stay there. No curfew. That's a bad sign. Ballplayers are human beings, and when human beings get to Florida they like to play. I would have felt much more comfortable if a curfew had been imposed on us. It would accomplish two things, in my opinion. One, it would help to make damn sure the guys were behaving and getting their rest. Two, it would help to emphasize the disciplined approach to our championship game. After all, it was for all the marbles in the American Football Conference and the right to play in the Super Bowl. There was a lot of everything riding on that Sunday.

I'm from the old school when it comes to handling athletes anyhow. I favor a tough disciplinarian attitude all the time, even during the exhibition games. And when I get that close to picking up all the chips, I sure as hell favor the tough approach. Pro ballplayers in any sport need this. I'll argue with anyone in the world on that. Ballplayers—some, not all, but enough to make a difference in your team's performance—will get away with whatever they can in the fun league. They may not be doing anything wrong morally, but they're not getting the rest and applying the concentration necessary to achieving success in any endeavor. And in any group of forty men away from home, this can be a problem if you do not take every necessary precaution. I was afraid we were not taking that precaution. I kept hoping I was wrong.

I couldn't even spend my first New Year's Eve as a married man with my wife. Marty is a good sport about these things, though, and we're grateful we got to spend most of Christmas day together. I had to practice that morning, and we left for Cleveland at six in the evening. But we had most of the day to enjoy our first Christmas. I gave Marty a sewing machine and she gave me a trophy case for my small mementoes—silver and gold footballs, rings and things that a ballplayer accumulates and likes to display in a tasteful way. She also gave me, in her usual thoughtful way, a glass painting of the chapel at Duke. It's beautiful, and so was the idea.

Mom and Dad came over from the farm at Leesburg and we enjoyed the kind of Christmas day everyone enjoys—good Christmas music on the record player, good conversation with the family, and a tasty ham dinner—Kentucky-style as cooked by the former Miss Boone, the new Mrs. Curtis.

We gave Dad a gun case, a big dark wood, glass-covered case that is a beautiful piece of furniture. For Mom we got a set of luggage and braided covers for her furniture, those early American covers that should look right at home in a pre-Civil War farmhouse.

With that trophy case I get a chance to show off my Super Bowl ring—from the game we won. Better than that, I can display my Duke graduation ring. I can't wear either of the rings because I can't get them over my finger. People tell me I should have them enlarged, but I've just never gotten around to it. I'll be glad to place that Duke class ring in a trophy case. I'm more proud of that than I am of my Super Bowl ring. I had to work a lot harder for the one from Duke.

Chapter *15*

I won't try to be a good loser, because I'm not. I'm not a sorehead either. But I won't say I don't care, or that's the old ball game, or wait till next year. I can't be casual about defeat. We lost, we got skunked, 21–0, and I am bitterly, bitterly disappointed. And what really galls me is we're better than Miami. I'll get a lot of heat for that statement, but I believe it. Three plays beat us—two bombs and an interception. Three plays out of 60 minutes.

We've outplayed Miami in all three games and won only one of them. In this one we had more first downs, more yards passing (even including their two bombs), more total yardage. And we had to punt only three times to their six.

People say the turning point came in the third quarter, when Dick Anderson intercepted a pass and went 60 yards for the score. They're wrong. It came earlier than that. It came at half time. As we were coming off the field at the end of the second period, I told Ray May, who was one of our co-captains for the game, that I wanted to speak to the team—without the coaches. I said, "I think it's necessary now. Get Unitas and Miller and tell them I want to say something to the rest of the team."

So we had our usual half-time get-together, when the coaches go over the mistakes and good plays of the first half—with an emphasis on the former, and in this case an absence of the latter. Then the coaches were asked to leave the room. They did. What I had to say didn't take long and it won't win any oratorical contest, but it was blunt, and in the short time that I spoke I was almost aching with hope—hope that somehow the words would work on all of us.

I said, "Some of you guys have been out playing around all week. Now we're going to lose this damn game if you don't make a drastic change. The offense keeps asking the defense to give them the ball. Well, we've given you the goddam ball about ten times so far and you haven't scored yet. You're lousy. Now do something about it."

Then John Mackey said something about being men but I didn't hear it, because I was still so damn preoccupied with what I had just said. No one else said anything. No one felt the need to argue with what I had just said. No one added anything to it, except for Mackey's comments. No one yelled defiance or obscenities. No one told me to go to hell. Nothing. That was the team's reaction. Nothing.

That's when we lost the game—and our championship—although no one outside the doors to our dressing room knew it. But those of us inside that room knew it—all of us. I just thought to myself, "There's no emotion here. We've lost this game." And we had. We didn't lose when Anderson picked up those five downfield blocks and went 60 yards. We lost it in our own dressing room, when the Dolphins weren't even in the same room with us.

I became involved in another of the season's conversation pieces. In the first half, Bob Griese dropped back to pass, but his receivers were covered. He took off on a run. He was running full tilt down the sidelines when I closed in on him and he headed for the out-of-bounds stripe—the same kind of thing I saw him do in those films of their game with the Patriots. I hit him when he was still several steps inbounds, but another of Rozelle's prize referees dropped the yellow flag on me and penalized us 15 yards because he thought I hit Griese out-of-bounds. It was one of those two times Miami crossed the 50-yard line.

Meanwhile, up in the broadcast booth, Curt Gowdy and Al DeRogatis are describing the action for the nationwide audience on NBC-TV. As soon as the flag is dropped, according to my friends, DeRogatis says, "That's not the way this game of football is played, Curt—on the field or off." Then, of course, the instant replay follows, only it shows Curtis and Griese are both well inbounds, and there isn't a thing wrong with the tackle. So what comment comes from the broadcast booth then? Not a sound.

Silence.

With Cosell I at least would have gotten something more.

So I've been accused of a dirty play in the live action, but when the instant replays show I did nothing wrong, there is silence. You figure it out. I thought about demanding a public apology after I heard about it, but that stamps you as a cry-baby, or people think it's sour grapes after you lose the game. So I decided to hell with it. But it goes back to what I said earlier about the incredible impact that announcers and reporters have on the lives of those men down on the field. They can praise you and help you earn more money next year. They can criticize you and give people the impression you're over the hill. Or, in this case, they can say something and be wrong but leave thousands or millions of viewers with the idea that you're a dirty ballplayer.

I did tackle Griese high, I admit to that. But admit is the wrong word, because on a high tackle there's nothing to admit. It's perfectly legal, ethical and acceptable. Even a clothesline shot is acceptable, and I didn't clothesline Griese, I hit him high—around the head and neck. And he shouldn't have been surprised. When a quarterback steps out onto that field, he's fair game. And when he tucks that ball inside his arm, he's the target and the defense aims at him.

The fact is that I looked to make sure where the sideline was before I tackled Griese. It was a championship game and I was not about to make a dumb mistake like hitting him out-of-bounds and costing my team 15 yards. So I checked to make sure, and the ref was right there beside me. I wonder if he saw the play the next day. I did, and Griese is still inbounds when I hit him.

I didn't want to hold back on Griese just because he's

the quarterback. Hell, he wasn't holding back. He came running at us full speed, then he shut down and tried to trot to the sidelines—same thing he did in the New England game after they intercepted that pass against him. He shuns the tackle, and they score on the return.

I don't try to hurt a guy seriously, but I'll be honest with you—I'm not upset if I shake them up. What the heck, it's a contact sport, isn't it? And one of the purposes of the game is to stop the man with the ball by tackling him, isn't it? That's what I did. If Griese doesn't like the pounding, he can get out of the game. That's what I'll do when the day comes that I can't take the pounding any more, either. In the meantime, while I'm on the field, I expect to pound and be pounded.

People assume, I know, that defensive players are the ones always dishing it out. They see the quarterback getting jarred, the runner dumped end-over-end, the punt returner dropped in his tracks. What they don't see, and I know it's understandable, are the linemen scratching the defensive linemen and the linebackers in the eyes. Or the centers punching us in the stomach as they come across the line. Not only do the offensive players do these things, they never get called on it by the officials. But you never hear us bitching about it. Then a quarterback gets one good, hard tackle—clean and legal—and there's a great big fuss.

Two comments about the incident tell you something. Griese admitted the big question in his mind was whether he was inbounds. He was, and the films prove it. And Shula said, "You hate to lose a quarterback on a hit out-of-bounds." The paper said that was all Shula would say about it, but he had something more to say to me about it.

On a play along the sidelines later, I had to do some fancy stepping to avoid tackling the ballcarrier—because he was out-of-bounds. As I hurtled the usual sideline mob, I went past Shula and he called me a bleeping cheap-shot artist. I was surprised and hurt. Also furious. I hadn't said anything to him. When he gave me that dirty crack, I almost hit him. It would have been the worst mistake of my life, but that's how mad it made me. I could see he was in a high emotional state. He was sensing victory more every minute. It could have been a nasty incident. But I walked away from it, thank goodness.

It hurt me as much as it made me angry. I like Don Shula, even after what he said. He's still my friend, and I still respect him as one of the outstanding coaches in the game. He did a lot for me, I owe him a great deal, and I'd play for him again in a minute.

A reporter asked me in the dressing room after the Miami game why I didn't argue with the ref about the call on my tackle of Griese. My answer to that is what more can I do? I've pleaded and complained and everything else, and so have a helluva lot of other guys, about the constant decline in the caliber of officiating in the NFL, but nothing ever happens to improve it. There is no court of appeals. The refs sure as hell are not improving their own performances, and Rozelle doesn't seem to be doing anything about it either—nothing that is producing improvement.

I have a theory which I think explains in part this problem of consistently poor officiating. My theory is that expansion shows in the officials as well as in the players. In both football and baseball, with the increase in the number of teams, you need more players to stock the teams. It also means more games, and that requires more officials to handle the greater number of games. So some guys are working as officials in pro football who maybe wouldn't be good enough if we didn't have so many vacancies to fill. So much for the officiating. It was the first thing I forgot in the offseason.

With the season over, I find my thoughts turning to what's ahead, for the Colts, for pro football, and for myself.

For the Colts, I'm not sure. It all depends on one man now—John Unitas. He's the guy we'll have our chips on come next September. He'll be 39 years old, and it's asking quite a bit for a guy that age to perform not only to an acceptable standard but to a championship standard. But he looked considerably improved in the final few games of our season, and maybe he can continue that improvement into the new season. Earl Morrall is gone now, sent to the Dolphins. I don't think he will help them that much, and I don't think his departure will hurt us that much. If John performs, there won't be any need for Earl anyhow. If John does perform, we'll be back in the Super Bowl—and I hope we go against a highly respected team. That way we can win—win the Super Bowl and win complete satisfaction, the kind that says you played like a champion in defeating a worthy opponent. I'm still waiting for that and playing for that. We can do it, but we'll have to want to.

I already want to.

For pro football, I think it's more of the same—more success, more recognition that professional football is now America's number one sport—and more criticism from the malcontents. I think that criticism—the vocal, unconstructive kind that faces the TV cameras and not the issues—

will continue to be heard about pro football as long as it is heard about the United States. As the nation's most popular sport today, it seems to follow that it will be the target of criticism in these years of protest.

I think the worst mistake pro football—and the American people—could make would be to overreact to that kind of criticism. The challenge is to maintain our stability, to keep our lives, our society and our sports on an even keel, instead of caving in under the heat from the loud Left, or the far Right.

This is not to say we should not change or continue to move ahead. It's change that has brought us—America and football—to the lives we lead today. Maybe those lives aren't all we would like them to be, and maybe change is needed, but not the kind of change that means change through force of arms and criticism through character assassination and instilling hate while calling for love. Violence under any name is still violence. Look at Northern Ireland. Hate is still hate, whether it is shouted from the Left or the Right.

We can live without it in the middle, even if those on the extremes can't talk without it. And we in America and in pro football can try to hold and preserve and improve what we have while feeling pity for the extremists—or ignoring them—but never yielding to them.

That is the great responsibility facing those of us in the vast center.

For myself, I can't be entirely selfish as the season ends. We did get into the playoffs. I did get to play all but one game despite a broken thumb. And I did get voted to the Pro Bowl for the third time as a linebacker. I can't minimize things like that. And I came through the season in good health and ready to tear 'em up next year, and I have to be thankful for that, too.

Then, too, this season gave me the opportunity to tell this story—a true story—about how things are in pro football, and how they are not. Through these pages I have been able to tell you the other side—the right side—about this great sport which is loved by so many Americans for what it is—a good game.

It's not an instrument to perpetuate rampant racism. It's not an evil back-room scheme conceived by shadowy villains running their hands through piles of money while holding their players in starvation and slavery. It's not a gang of doped-up sex fiends playing in wild abandon.

It's a game. A source of immense pleasure to millions of Americans, a constructive, healthy, fun game, and no one—no one—can change that.

Pro football is a decent game, played by decent people, operated by decent people, and watched and enjoyed by decent people.

That's the truth.